Big Book of
Dishcloths, Pot Holders & Scrubbies™

General Information

Many of the products used in this pattern book can be purchased from local craft, fabric and variety stores, or from the Annie's Attic Needlecraft Catalog (see Customer Service information on page 63).

Contents

Paint the Town

DESIGN BY **JEAN LEINHAUSER**

SKILL LEVEL

EASY

FINISHED SIZE
10½ inches square

MATERIALS
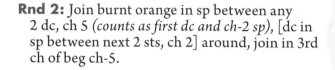

- Pisgah Yarn and Dyeing Co., Inc. Peaches & Crème medium (worsted) weight yarn (2½ oz/ 122 yds/70g per ball):
  1 ball each #19 peacock and #13 burnt orange
- Size G/6/4mm crochet hook or size needed to obtain gauge

GAUGE
4 dc = 1 inch; 2 dc rows = 1 inch

PATTERN NOTES
Chain-3 at beginning of round counts as first double crochet unless otherwise stated.

Join with slip stitch unless otherwise stated.

SPECIAL STITCH
Long double crochet (long dc): Yo, insert hook in corresponding st on rnd 9, pull up long lp, [yo, pull through 2 lps on hook] twice.

INSTRUCTIONS
DISHCLOTH
Rnd 1: With peacock, ch 8, **join** (see Pattern Notes) in beg ch to form ring, **ch 3** (see Pattern Notes), 15 dc in ring, join in 3rd ch of beg ch-3. Fasten off. (16 dc)

Rnd 2: Join burnt orange in sp between any 2 dc, ch 5 (counts as first dc and ch-2 sp), [dc in sp between next 2 sts, ch 2] around, join in 3rd ch of beg ch-5.

Rnd 3: Sl st in next ch-2 sp, ch 3, 2 dc in same sp, ch 1, [3 dc in next ch-2 sp, ch 1] around, join in 3rd ch of beg ch-3. Fasten off. (48 dc)

Rnd 4: Join peacock with sc in any ch-1 sp, ch 5, sc in next ch sp, *[ch 3, sc in next ch sp] 3 times, ch 5**, sc in next ch sp, rep from * around, ending last rep at **, join in beg sc.

Rnd 5: (Sl st, ch 3, 2 dc, ch 2, 3 dc) in first ch sp, 3 dc in each of next 3 ch sps, *(3 dc, ch 2, 3 dc) in next ch sp, 3 dc in each of next 3 ch sps, rep from * around, join in 3rd ch of beg ch-3.

Rnd 6: Sl st in each of next 2 sts, sl st in next ch sp, ch 4 (counts as first tr), 2 tr in same sp, *[dc in sp between next 2 sts] 5 times, [hdc in sp between next 2 sts] 4 times, [dc in sp between next 2 sts] 5 times**, 3 tr in next ch sp, rep from * around, ending last rep at **, join in 4th ch of beg ch-4. Fasten off.

Rnd 7: Join burnt orange with sc in any center corner tr, 2 sc in same st, *2 sc in sp between last worked st and next st, [sc in sp between next 2 sts] 15 times, 2 sc in next sp between next 2 sts**, 3 sc in next st, rep from * around, ending last rep at **, join in beg sc.

Rnd 8: Ch 3, dc in each st around with (dc, ch 3, dc) in each corner st, join in 3rd ch of beg ch-3. Fasten off.

Rnd 9: Working this rnd in **back lps** *(see Stitch Guide)*, join peacock with sc in center ch of any corner ch sp, 2 sc in same ch, sc in each ch and in each st around with 3 sc in center ch of each center corner ch sp, join in beg sc.

Rnd 10: Ch 1, sc in first st, ch 3, sk next st, [sc in next st, ch 3, sk next st] around, join in beg sc.

Rnd 11: Sl st in next ch sp, ch 4 *(counts as first tr)*, 4 tr in same sp, *sc in next ch sp, [5 dc in next ch sp, sc in next ch sp] 6 times**, 5 tr in next ch sp, rep from * around, ending last rep at **, join in 4th ch of beg ch-4. Fasten off.

Rnd 12: Join burnt orange in first tr of any 5-tr corner group, ch 3, dc in next tr, *3 dc in next tr, dc in each of next 2 tr, working over next sc, **long dc** *(see Special Stitch)*, [dc in each of next 5 dc, working over next sc, long dc] 6 times**, dc in each of next 2 tr, rep from * around ending last rep at **, join in 3rd ch of beg ch-3. Fasten off. ∎

Dainty Daffodil
Scrubbie

DESIGN BY **SHERI L. JACOBSON**

SKILL LEVEL

EASY

FINISHED SIZE
5½ inches across

MATERIALS
- Pisgah Yarn and Dyeing Co., Inc. Peaches & Crème medium (worsted) weight yarn (2½ oz/ 122 yds/70g per ball):
  1 ball each #1 white, #10 yellow, #11 sunburst and #62 emerald
- Size G/6/4mm crochet hook or size needed to obtain gauge
- Tapestry needle
- 1-inch plastic ring
- Safety pins
- Plastic mesh pot scrubber

GAUGE
4 dc = 1 inch; 2 dc rows = 1 inch

PATTERN NOTES
Join with slip stitch as indicated unless otherwise stated.

Chain-3 at beginning of round counts as first double crochet unless otherwise stated.

INSTRUCTIONS
SCRUBBIE
Rnd 1: With yellow, ch 3, **join** (see Pattern Notes) in beg ch to form ring, **ch 3** (see Pattern Notes), 14 dc in ring, join in 3rd ch of beg ch-3, **turn**. (15 dc)

Rnd 2: Working this rnd in **back lps** (see Stitch Guide), ch 1, sc in each st around, join in beg sc. (15 sc)

Rnd 3: Ch 1, sc in each st around, join in beg sc.

Rnd 4: Ch 1, sc in each st around, join in beg sc, **turn**.

Rnd 5: Ch 3, [sl st in next st, ch 3] around, join in joining sl st of last rnd. Fasten off.

Rnd 6: With last rnd facing, working in rem lps of rnd 1, join white in any st, ch 3, dc in same st, 2 dc in each st around, join in 3rd ch of beg ch 3. (30 dc)

Rnd 7: Ch 3, dc in same st, dc in next st, 2 dc in next st, dc in next st, ch 1, sk next st, *[2 dc in next st, dc in next st] twice, ch 1, sk next st, rep from * around, join in 3rd ch of beg ch-3. (36 dc, 6 ch-1 sps)

Rnd 8: Ch 1, sc in first st, *2 dc in next st, (dc, tr) in next st, ch 2, sl st in top of last tr made, (tr dc) in next st, 2 dc in next st, sc in next st, sl st in next ch sp**, sc in next st, rep from * around, ending last rep at **, join in beg sc. Fasten off.

Rnd 9: Working behind last 2 rnds, join emerald in any sk st on rnd 6, ch 9 *(counts as first dc and ch-6 sp)*, [dc in next sk st, ch 6] around, join in 3rd ch of beg ch-9. *(6 ch-6 sps)*

Note: Using safety pins, pin rnd 9 to outer edge of plastic scrubber. Remove pins when needed as you work.

Rnd 10: Ch 1, *[insert hook in next ch on rnd 9 and under 5 or 6 plastic mesh strands, yo, pull lp through, complete as sc] 6 times, sk in next dc, rep from * around, join in beg sc. Fasten off.

For **stamens**, thread 6 inches of sunburst in tapestry needle and run through bottom of 1 dc at center of rnd 1; remove needle and tie strand in knot. Tie knot in each end of strand 1 inch from Flower and trim excess close to knot. Rep with another 6-inch strand in st opposite first one.

LEAF
MAKE 2.
With emerald, ch 12, sc in 2nd ch from hook, sc in next ch, hdc in each of next 2 chs, dc in each of last 7 chs. Fasten off, leaving long strand for sewing.

Sew Leaves side by side to last rnd of Scrubbie.

HANGER
Join emerald with **sc in plastic ring** *(see Fig. 1)*, 19 sc in ring, join in beg sc. Fasten off, leaving long strand for sewing.

Fig. 1
Single Crochet Over Ring

Sew to last rnd of Scrubbie opposite Leaves. ■

Daffodil
Pot Holder

DESIGN BY **DIANE STONE**

SKILL LEVEL

EASY

FINISHED SIZE
6½ inches in diameter, not including hanging lp

MATERIALS
- Size 10 crochet cotton:
  - 150 yds cream
  - 25 yds lilac
  - 15 yds gold
  - 10 yds green
- Size 1/2.25mm steel crochet hook or size needed to obtain gauge
- Tapestry needle
- 1-inch plastic ring

GAUGE
With 2 strands held tog: Daffodil = 2 inches across; rnds 1 and 2 of Back = 2¼ inches across

PATTERN NOTES
Join with slip stitch as indicated unless otherwise stated.

Chain-3 at beginning of round counts as first double crochet unless otherwise stated.

Use 2 strands crochet cotton held together throughout unless otherwise stated.

SPECIAL STITCHES
Picot: Ch 1, sl st in top of last st made.

Beginning shell (beg shell): Ch 3, (2 dc, ch 2, 3 dc) in same place.

Shell: (3 dc, ch 2, 3 dc) in indicated place.

Long double crochet (long dc): Yo, insert hook in indicated place, yo, pull up long lp, [yo, pull through 2 lps on hook] twice.

INSTRUCTIONS
POT HOLDER
DAFFODIL
Rnd 1: With gold, ch 2, 12 sc in 2nd ch from hook, **join** *(see Pattern Notes)* in beg sc. *(12 sc)*

Rnd 2: Working this rnd in **front lps** *(see Stitch Guide)*, **ch 3** *(see Pattern Notes)*, dc in each st around, join in 3rd ch of beg ch-3. *(12 dc)*

Rnd 3: Ch 1, [sl st in next st, ch 1] around, join in joining sl st of last rnd. Fasten off.

Rnd 4: For **petals**, working behind rnd 2 in rem **back lps** *(see Stitch Guide)* of rnd 1, join gold in any st of rnd 1, (ch 3, tr, dtr, **picot**—*see Special Stitches*, tr, ch 3, sl st) in same st, sk next st, *(sl st, ch 3, tr, dtr, picot, tr ch 3, sl st) in next st, sk next st, rep from * around, join in beg sl st. Fasten off. *(6 petals)*

Rnd 5: Working behind last rnd in back lps of sk sts on rnd 1, join cream with sc in any sk st, ch 3, [sc in next sk st, ch 3] around, join in beg sc. *(6 ch sps)*

Rnd 6: Ch 3, 3 dc in next ch sp, [dc in next st, 3 dc in next ch sp] round, join in 3rd ch of beg ch-3. *(24 dc)*

Rnd 7: Ch 3, 2 dc in next st, [dc in next st, 2 dc in next st] around, join in 3rd ch of beg ch-3. *(36 dc)*

Rnd 8: **Beg shell** (*see Special Stitches*) in first st, sk next 2 sts, [**shell** (*see Special Stitches*) in next st, sk next 2 sts] around, join in 3rd ch of beg ch-3. (*12 shells*)

Rnd 9: Sl st in each of next 2 sts, (sl st, beg shell) in next ch sp, shell in ch sp of each shell around, join in 3rd ch of beg ch-3.

Rnd 10: Sl st in each of next 2 sts, (sl st, beg shell) in next ch sp, ch 1, [shell in next shell, ch 1] around, join in 3rd ch of beg ch-3.

Rnd 11: Sl st in each of next 2 sts, (sl st, beg shell) in next ch sp, ch 2, [shell in next shell, ch 2] around, join in 3rd ch of beg ch-3. Fasten off.

LEAF
MAKE 6.
With green, ch 4, sc in 2nd ch from hook, hdc in next ch, 5 dc in last ch, working on opposite side of ch, hdc in next ch, sc in last ch, ch 2, join in beg sc. Fasten off.

Working behind petals, sew Leaves between petals (*see photo*). Tack back of petals to rnd 6.

BACK
Rnd 1: With cream, ch 5, 23 tr in 5th ch from hook (*first 4 chs count as first tr*), join in 4th ch of beg ch-4. (*24 tr*)

Rnd 2: Ch 3, 2 dc in next st, [dc in next st, 2 dc in next st] around, join in 3rd ch of beg ch-3. (*36 dc*)

Rnd 3: Ch 3, dc in next st, 2 dc in next st, [dc in each of next 2 sts, 2 dc in next st] around, join in 3rd ch of beg ch-3. (*48 dc*)

Rnd 4: Ch 3, dc in each of next 2 sts, 2 dc in next st, [dc in each of next 3 sts, 2 dc in next st] around, join in 3rd ch of beg ch-3. (*60 dc*)

Rnd 5: Ch 3, dc in each of next 3 sts, 2 dc in next st, [dc in each of next 4 sts, 2 dc in next st] around, join in 3rd ch of beg ch-3. (*72 dc*)

Rnd 6: Ch 1, sc in each st around, join in beg sc.

Rnd 7: Beg shell in first st, ch 2, sk next 5 sts, [shell in next st, ch 2, sk next 5 sts] around, join in 3rd ch of beg ch-3. Fasten off. (*12 shells*)

Rnd 8: Holding Front and Back WS tog with Front facing, matching sts, working through both thicknesses, join lilac in any shell, ch 3, 9 dc in same shell, [*working over next ch sp, **long dc** (*see Special Stitches*) in next ch sp on rnd before last on Front and in 3rd sc of sk 5-sc group on rnd before last of Back at same time*, 10 dc in next shell on last rnd] 11 times, rep between * once, for **hanging lp**, holding plastic ring close to work, 24 **sc around ring** (*see Fig. 1*), join in beg sc around ring, join in 3rd ch of beg ch-3 on last rnd. Fasten off.

Fig. 1
Single Crochet Over Ring

Row 9: Now working in rows, join green in first st, [ch 1, sl st in next st] around, leaving last long dc and sts on ring unworked. Fasten off. ■

Housewarming
Pot Holder

DESIGN BY **JOCELYN SASS**

SKILL LEVEL

EASY

FINISHED SIZE
8 x 8½ inches, including chimney

MATERIALS
- Pisgah Yarn and Dyeing Co., Inc. Peaches & Crème medium (worsted) weight yarn (2½ oz/ 122 yds/70g per ball):
  2 balls #24 Williamsburg blue
  1 ball each #48 mauve and #4 ecru
- Size G/6/4mm crochet hook or size needed to obtain gauge
- Tapestry needle

4

MEDIUM

GAUGE
4 sc = 1 inch; 4 sc rows = 1 inch

PATTERN NOTES
When **changing colors** *(see Stitch Guide)*, always drop unused color to back side of work. Do not carry dropped color across back of work; use a separate ball of yarn for each color section. Fasten off each color when no longer needed.

Work odd-numbered rows from right to left and even-numbered rows from left to right.

Each square on chart counts as 1 single crochet.

INSTRUCTIONS
FRONT
Row 1: With Williamsburg blue, ch 30, sc in 2nd ch from hook and in each of next 18 chs, **changing color** *(see Pattern Notes)* to mauve in last st, sc in each of next 7 chs, changing to Williamsburg blue in last st, sc in each of last 3 sts, turn. *(29 sc)*

Rows 2–18: Ch 1, sc in each st across, changing colors according to House Chart, turn.

Rows 19–27: Ch 1, **sc dec** *(see Stitch Guide)* in first 2 sts, sc in each st across to last 2 sts, sc dec in last 2 sts, turn. *(11 sc at end of last row)*

Rnd 28: Now working in rnds around outer edge, ch 1, sc in each st and in end of each row around with 3 sc in each corner, changing colors as need to match piece, join with sl st in beg sc. Fasten off.

With ecru, using **backstitch** *(see Fig. 1)* and **French knot** *(see Fig. 2)*, embroider Front according to House Chart.

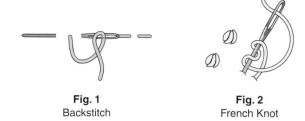

Fig. 1
Backstitch

Fig. 2
French Knot

BACK
Row 1: With Williamsburg blue, ch 30, sc in 2nd ch from hook and in each ch across, turn. *(29 sc)*

Rows 2–18: Ch 1, sc in each st across, turn.

Rows 19–27: Ch 1, sc dec in first 2 sts, sc in each st across to last 2 sts, sc dec in last 2 sts, turn. *(11 sc at end of last row)*

Rnd 28: Now working in rnds around outer edge, ch 1, sc in each st and in end of each row around with 3 sc in each corner, join with sl st in beg sc. Fasten off.

Hold Front and Back WS tog with Front facing, matching sts, working through both thicknesses in **back lps** *(see Stitch Guide)*, sl st tog, changing colors as needed to match piece.

CHIMNEY

Row 1: With Williamsburg blue, ch 3, sc in 2nd ch from hook and in last ch, turn. *(2 sc)*

Rows 2–5: Ch 1, sc in each st across, turn. **Do not turn** at end of last row.

Rnd 6: Now working in rnds, ch 1, sc in each st and in end of each row around with 3 sc in each corner, join in beg sc. Fasten off.

Sew to 1 side of roof on Front as shown. ∎

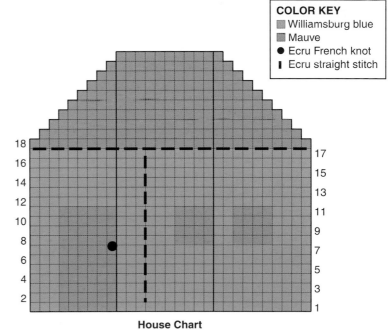

COLOR KEY
- Williamsburg blue
- Mauve
- ● Ecru French knot
- I Ecru straight stitch

House Chart

Cluster Dishcloth

DESIGN BY SHERI L. JACOBSON

SKILL LEVEL

EASY

FINISHED SIZE
9 inches square

MATERIALS
- Pisgah Yarn and Dyeing Co., Inc. Peaches & Crème medium (worsted) weight yarn (2½ oz/ 122 yds/70g per ball):
  - 2 balls #4 ecru
  - 1 ball #52 light sage
- Size H/8/5mm crochet hook or size needed to obtain gauge

GAUGE
5 cls and 4 ch-1 sps = 3 inches; 7 cl rows and sc rows = 6 inches

PATTERN NOTE
Chain-3 at beginning of row counts as first double crochet unless otherwise stated.

SPECIAL STITCH
Cluster (cl): Yo, insert hook in next ch sp, yo, pull lp through, yo, pull through 2 lps on hook, [yo, insert hook in same ch sp, yo, pull lp through, yo, pull through 2 lps on hook] twice, yo, pull through all 4 lps on hook.

INSTRUCTIONS
DISHCLOTH
Row 1: With ecru, ch 26, sc in 2nd ch from hook, [ch 1, sk next ch, sc in next ch] across, turn. *(13 sc, 12 ch sps)*

Row 2 (RS): Ch 3 *(see Pattern Note)*, **cl** *(see Special Stitch)* in next ch sp, [ch 1, cl in next ch sp] across to last st, dc in last st, turn. *(12 cls, 11 ch sps, 2 dc)*

Row 3: Ch 1, sc in first st, [ch 1, sc in next ch sp] across to last st, ch 1, sc in last st, turn. *(13 sc, 12 ch sps)*

Rows 4–17: [Rep rows 2 and 3 alternately] 7 times.

Rnd 18: Now working in rnds, ch 1, 3 sc in first st, sc in each st and in each ch sp across with 3 sc in last st, evenly sp 23 sc across ends of rows, working in starting ch on opposite side of row 1, 3 sc in first ch, sc in each ch across with 3 sc in last ch, evenly sp 23 sc across ends of rows, join with sl st in beg sc. Fasten off. *(25 sc across each side between corner sc)*

Rnd 19: Join light sage with sc in first center corner st, 2 sc in same st, sc in each st around with 3 sc in each center corner st, join with sl st in beg sc. Fasten off. *(27 sc across each side between corner sts)*

Rnd 20: Join ecru with sc in first center corner st, sc in same st, sc in each st around with 3 sc in each center corner st, sc in same st as beg sc, join with sl st in beg sc. Fasten off. ■

Butterfly
Dishcloth

DESIGN BY **SUE CHILDRESS**

SKILL LEVEL

EASY

FINISHED SIZE
6 inches square

MATERIALS
- Pisgah Yarn and Dyeing Co., Inc. Peaches & Crème medium (worsted) weight yarn (2 oz/ 98 yds/56g per ball):
    - 1 ball #147 shaded brown
- Size G/6/4mm crochet hook or size needed to obtain gauge

GAUGE
4 dc = 1 inch; 2 dc rows = 1 inch

PATTERN NOTES
Join with slip stitch as indicated unless otherwise stated.

Chain-3 at beginning of row counts as first double crochet unless otherwise stated.

Chain-4 at beginning of row counts as first double crochet and chain-1 space unless otherwise stated.

SPECIAL STITCHES
V-stitch (V-st): (Dc, ch 1, dc) in next ch sp.

Cluster (cl): Yo, insert hook in indicated place, yo, pull lp through, yo, pull through 2 lps on hook, yo, insert hook in same place, yo, pull lp through, yo, pull through 2 lps on hook, yo, pull through all 3 lps on hook.

INSTRUCTIONS
DISHCLOTH
Row 1: Ch 28, sc in 2nd ch from hook, ch 2, sk next ch, sc in next ch, [sk next 3 chs, (3 tr, ch 4, sc) in next ch, ch 2, sk next ch, (sc, ch 4, 3 tr) in next ch, sk next 3 chs, sc in next ch, ch 2, sk next ch, sc in next ch] across, turn.

Row 2: Ch 4 (see Pattern Notes), dc in first ch-2 sp, ch 1, sk next 3 tr, sc in top of next ch-4, ch 2, **cl** (see Special Stitches) in next ch-2 sp, ch 2, sc in top of next ch-4, ch 1, sk next 3 tr, [**V-st** (see Special Stitches) in next ch-2 sp, ch 1, sk next 3 tr, sc in top of next ch-4, ch 2, cl in next ch-2 sp, ch 2, sc in top of next ch-4, ch 1, sk next 3 tr] across to last ch-2 sp, dc in last ch-2 sp, ch 1, dc in last st, turn.

Rnd 3: Ch 1, sc in same st, ch 2, sk next ch-1 sp, *sc in next ch-1 sp, (3 tr, ch 4, sc) in next ch-2 sp, ch 2, sk next cl, (sc, ch 4, 3 tr) in next ch-2 sp, sc in next ch-1 sp**, ch 2, sk next V-st, rep from * across, ending last rep at **, ch 2, sk next dc, sc in 3rd ch of last ch-4, turn.

Rows 4–11: [Rep rows 2 and 3 alternately] 4 times.

Row 12: Rep row 2, **do not turn**.

Rnd 13: Now working in rnds around outer edge, ch 1, 2 sc in end of each dc row, sc in end of each sc row, sc in each st and sc in each ch around with 3 sc in each corner, join in beg sc. *(98 sc)*

Rnd 14: Ch 1, sc in first st, sk next 2 sts, 5 dc in next st, sk next 2 sts, [sc in next st, sk next st, 5 dc in next st, sk next st] around, join in beg sc. Fasten off. ■

Poppy
SCRUBBIE
DESIGN BY **SHERI L. JACOBSON**

SKILL LEVEL

EASY

FINISHED SIZE
5 inches in diameter

MATERIALS
- Pisgah Yarn and Dyeing Co., Inc. Peaches & Crème medium (worsted) weight yarn (2½ oz/ 122 yds/70g per ball):
  1 ball each #95 red, #2 black and #63 hunter
- Size G/6/4mm crochet hook or size needed to obtain gauge
- Tapestry needle
- 1-inch plastic ring
- Safety pins
- Plastic mesh pot scrubber

GAUGE
Rnds 1–3 = 2½ inches across

PATTERN NOTES
Join with slip stitch as indicated unless otherwise stated.

Chain-3 at beginning of round counts as first double crochet unless otherwise stated.

When **changing colors** (*see Stitch Guide*), always drop unused color to wrong side of work, carry along back of work, picking up when needed. Fasten off each color when no longer needed.

INSTRUCTIONS
SCRUBBIE
Rnd 1: With black, ch 3, **join** (*see Pattern Notes*) in beg ch to form ring, ch 2, drop lp from hook, with hunter, pull through lp on hook (*first 3 chs count as first dc*), dc in ring, **changing color** (*see Pattern Notes*) to black, [dc in ring, changing to hunter, dc in ring, changing to black] 6 times, join in 3rd ch of beg 3 chs. *(14 dc)*

Rnd 2: Working this rnd in **front lps** (*see Stitch Guide*), ch 3, [sl st in next st, ch 3] around, join in joining sl st of last rnd. Fasten off.

Rnd 3: Working this rnd in **back lps** (*see Stitch Guide*) of rnd 1, join red in any st, **ch 3** (*see Pattern Notes*) dc in same st, 2 dc in each st around to last st, dc in last st, join in front lp of 3rd ch of beg ch-3. (*27 dc*)

Rnd 4: Working this rnd in front lps, ch 4, tr in same st, *2 tr in each of next 5 sts, (tr, ch 4, sl st) in next st, sl st in each of next 2 sts**, (sl st, ch 4, tr) in next st, rep from * around, ending last rep at **, join in back lp of 3rd ch of beg ch-3 on last rnd.

Rnd 5: Working in back lps of rnd 3, ch 3, dc in same st, *2 dc in next st, [dc in next st, 2 dc in next st] 6 times, rep from *, join in front lp of 3rd ch of beg ch-3. (*42 dc*)

Rnd 6: Working this rnd in front lps, ch 3, dc in same st, dc in next st, 2 dc in next st, *dc in next st, (dc, ch 3, sl st) in next st, sl st in each of next 3 sts, (sl st, ch 3, dc) in next st**, [dc in next st, 2 dc in next st] 4 times, rep from * twice, ending last rep at **, dc in next st, [2 dc in next st, dc in next st] twice, join in back lp of 3rd ch of beg ch-3 on last rnd.

Note: Using safety pins, pin rnd 6 to outer edge of plastic scrubber. Remove pins when needed as you work.

Rnd 7: Working this rnd in back lps of rnd 5, ch 1, insert hook in first st and under 5 or 6 plastic mesh strands, yo, complete as sc, [insert hook in next st and under 5 or 6 plastic mesh strands, yo, complete as sc] around, join in beg sc. Fasten off.

LEAF
MAKE 2.
Row 1: With hunter, ch 6, sc in 2nd ch from hook and in each ch across, turn. (*5 sc*)

Rows 2–4: Ch 4, sc in 2nd ch from hook, sc in each of next 2 chs, sc in each of next 2 sts, leaving rem sts unworked, turn. (*5 sc*)

Rows 5 & 6: Ch 3, sc in 2nd ch from hook, sc in next ch, sc in each of next 2 sts, leaving rem sts unworked, turn. (*4 sc*)

Row 7: Ch 4, sc in 2nd ch from hook, sc in each of next 2 chs, sl st in next st, leaving rem sts unworked. Fasten off.

Sew Leaves side by side to last rnd of Scrubbie.

HANGER
Join hunter with **sc in plastic ring** (*see Fig. 1*), 19 sc in ring, join in beg sc. Fasten off, leaving long strand for sewing.

Sew to last rnd of Scrubbie opposite Leaves. ∎

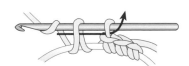

Fig. 1
Single Crochet Over Ring

Rose & Kiwi
Pot Holder

DESIGN BY JUDY TEAGUE TREECE

SKILL LEVEL

EASY

FINISHED SIZE
6½ inch square, not including hanging lp

MATERIALS
- Fine (sport) cotton yarn:
  150 yds rose
  100 yds kiwi
- Size 0/2.50mm steel crochet hook
  or size needed to obtain gauge

2
FINE

GAUGE
Rnds 1–5 of Front = 3¼ inches square

PATTERN NOTES
Join with slip stitch as indicated unless
otherwise stated.

Chain-3 at beginning of round counts as first
double crochet unless otherwise stated.

Chain-4 at beginning of round counts as first
double crochet and chain-1 space unless
otherwise stated.

SPECIAL STITCHES
3-double crochet cluster (3-dc cl): Yo, insert hook
in next st, yo, pull lp through, yo, pull through
2 lps on hook, [yo, insert hook in same st, yo,
pull lp through, yo, pull through 2 lps on hook]
twice, yo, pull through all 4 lps on hook.

4-double crochet cluster (4-dc cl): Yo, insert hook
in next st, yo, pull lp through, yo, pull through
2 lps on hook, [yo, insert hook in same st, yo,
pull lp through, yo, pull through 2 lps on hook]
three times, yo, pull through all 5 lps on hook.

INSTRUCTIONS
FRONT
Rnd 1: With rose, ch 5, **join** (see Pattern Notes) in
beg ch to form ring, **ch 3** (see Pattern Notes), 15
dc in ring, join in 3rd ch of beg ch-3. (16 dc)

Rnd 2 (RS): Ch 1, sc in first st, for **petal**, (sc,
ch 3, **3-dc cl**—see Special Stitches, ch 3, sc) in
next st, *sc in next st, (sc, ch 3, 3-dc cl, ch 3, sc)
in next st, rep from * around, join in beg sc.
(8 petals, 8 sc)

Rnd 3: Ch 1, sc in first st, ch 5, sk next petal,
[sc in next st between petals, ch 5, sk next
petal] around, join in beg sc, **turn.** Fasten
off. (8 ch sps)

Rnd 4: Join kiwi in first ch sp, ch 3, (3 dc, ch 2, 4
dc) in same sp, 6 dc in next ch sp, *(4 dc, ch 2, 4
dc) in next ch sp, 6 dc in next ch sp, rep from *
around, join in 3rd ch of beg ch-3. (14 dc across
each side between corner ch sps)

Rnd 5: Ch 3, dc in each st around with (2 dc, ch
2, 2 dc) in each ch sp, join in 3rd ch of beg ch-3.
Fasten off. (18 dc across each side between corner
ch sps)

Rnd 6: Join rose in any ch sp, ch 3, (dc, ch 2, 2
dc) in same sp, [ch 2, sk next 2 sts, **4-dc cl** (see

Special Stitches) in next st] 6 times, ch 2, *(2 dc, ch 2, 2 dc) in next ch sp, [ch 2, sk next 2 sts, 4-dc cl in next st] 6 times, ch 2, rep from * around, join in 3rd ch of beg ch-3. Fasten off. *(7 ch sps across each side between corner ch sps)*

Rnd 7: Join kiwi in first corner ch sp, ch 3, (dc, ch 2, 2 dc) in same sp, ch 2, [4-dc cl in next ch sp, ch 2] across to next corner ch sp, *(2 dc, ch 2, 2 dc) in next ch sp, ch 2, [4-dc cl in next ch sp, ch 2] across to next corner ch sp, rep from * around, join in 3rd ch of beg ch-3. *(8 ch sps across each side between corner ch sps)*

Rnds 8 & 9: Sl st in next st, sl st in next ch sp, ch 3, (dc, ch 2, 2 dc) in same sp, ch 2, [4-dc cl in next ch sp, ch 2] across to next corner ch sp, *(2 dc, ch 2, 2 dc) in next ch sp, ch 2, [4-dc cl in next ch sp, ch 2] across to next corner ch sp, rep from * around, join in 3rd ch of beg ch-3. Fasten off at end of last rnd. *(10-ch sps across each side between corner ch sps at end of last rnd)*

BACK

Rnd 1: With rose, ch 5, join in beg ch to form ring, ch 3, 15 dc in ring, join in 3rd ch of beg ch-3. *(16 dc)*

Rnd 2: Ch 3, dc in same st, 2 dc in each st around, join in 3rd ch of beg ch-3. *(32 dc)*

Rnd 3: Ch 3, (dc, ch 2, 2 dc) in same st, dc in each of next 7 sts, *(2 dc, ch 2, 2 dc) in next st, dc in each of next 7 sts, rep from * around, join in 3rd ch of beg ch-3. *(11 dc across each side between ch sps)*

Rnds 4–8: Ch 3, dc in each st around with (2 dc, ch 2, 2 dc) in each ch sp, join in 3rd ch of beg ch-3. Fasten off at end of last rnd. *(31 dc across each side between ch sps at end of last rnd)*

Holding Front and Back WS tog with Front facing, matching sts, working through both thicknesses, join rose with sc in any corner ch sp, sc in same sp, sc evenly sp around outer edge with 4 sc in each corner ch sp, 2 sc in same sp as first sc, join in beg sc, for **hanging lp**, ch 16, sl st in same st, **turn**, 24 sc in ch-16 lp, sl st in same st on Pot Holder. Fasten off. ∎

Kiwi & White Pot Holder
DESIGN BY **JUDY TEAGUE TREECE**

SKILL LEVEL

EASY

FINISHED SIZE
7½ inches across, not including hanging lp

MATERIALS
- Fine (sport) cotton yarn:
  150 yds kiwi
  50 yds white
- Size 0/2.50mm steel crochet hook or size needed to obtain gauge

GAUGE
Rnds 1–5 of Front = 3½ inches across

PATTERN NOTES
Join with slip stitch as indicated unless otherwise stated.

Chain-3 at beginning of round counts as first double crochet unless otherwise stated.

Chain-4 at beginning of round counts as first double crochet and chain-1 space unless otherwise stated.

SPECIAL STITCH
Long double crochet (long dc): Yo, insert hook in next st on rnd before last, yo, pull up long lp, [yo, pull through 2 lps on hook] twice.

INSTRUCTIONS
FRONT
Rnd 1: With kiwi, ch 4, **join** *(see Pattern Notes)* in beg ch to form ring, ch 1, 8 sc in ring, join in beg sc. *(8 sc)*

Rnd 2: Ch 3 *(see Pattern Notes)*, 2 dc in same st, 3 dc in each st around, join in 3rd ch of beg ch-3. *(24 dc)*

Rnd 3: **Ch 4** *(see Pattern Notes)*, dc in same st, ch 1, sk next st, *(dc, ch 1, dc) in next st, ch 1, sk next st, rep from * around, join in 3rd ch of beg ch-4. Fasten off. *(24 dc, 24 ch sps)*

Rnd 4: Join white with sc in first ch sp, sc in same sp, working over next ch sp, **long dc** *(see Special Stitch)* in corresponding sk st on rnd before last, [2 sc in next ch sp on last rnd, working over next ch sp, long dc in corresponding sk st on rnd before last] around, join in beg sc. *(24 sc, 12 long dc)*

Rnd 5: Ch 4, dc in same st, (dc, ch 1, dc) in next st, ch 1, sk next st, *(dc, ch 1, dc) in each of next 2 sts, ch 1, sk next st, rep from * around, join in 3rd ch of beg ch-4. Fasten off. *(36 ch sps)*

Rnd 6: Join kiwi with sc in first ch sp, sc in same sp, 2 sc in next ch sp, working over next ch sp, long dc in corresponding sk st on rnd before last, [2 sc in each of next 2 ch sps, working over next ch sp, long dc in corresponding sk st on rnd before last] around, join in beg sc. *(48 sc, 12 long dc)*

Rnd 7: Ch 4, dc in same st, dc in next st, (dc, ch 1, dc) in next st, dc next st, ch 1, sk next st, *[(dc, ch 1 dc) in next st, dc in next st] twice, ch 1, sk next st, rep from * around, join in beg sc. Fasten off. *(72 dc, 36 ch sps)*

Rnd 8: Join white with sc in first ch sp, sc in same sp, *ch 1, sk next 3 sts, 2 sc in next ch sp, ch 1, sk next 2 sts, working over next ch sp, long dc in corresponding sk st on rnd before last, ch 1, sk next st**, 2 sc in next ch sp, rep from * around, ending last rep at **, join in beg sc. *(48 sc, 36 ch sps, 12 long dc)*

Rnd 9: Ch 4, dc in same st, (dc, ch 1, dc) in next st, sk next ch sp, (dc, ch 1, dc) in each of next 2 sts, ch 1, sk next ch sp, dc in next st, ch 1, sk next ch sp, *(dc, ch 1, dc) in each of next 2 sts, sk next ch sp, (dc, ch 1, dc) in each of next 2 sts, ch 1, sk next ch sp, dc in next st, ch 1, sk next ch sp, rep from * around, join in 3rd ch of beg ch-4. Fasten off. *(72 ch sps)*

Rnd 10: Join kiwi with sc in first ch sp, sc in same sp, ch 1, [2 sc in next ch sp, ch 1] 3 times, [working over next ch sp, long dc in corresponding ch sp on rnd before last, ch 1] twice, *[2 sc in next ch sp, ch 1] 4 times, [working over next ch sp, long dc in corresponding ch sp on rnd before last, ch 1] twice, rep from * around, join in beg sc. *(96 sc, 72 ch sps, 24 long dc)*

Rnd 11: Ch 1, sk ch sps, sc in each st around, join in beg sc. Fasten off. *(120 sc)*

BACK

Rnd 1: With kiwi, ch 4, join in beg ch to form ring, ch 1, 8 sc in ring, join in beg sc. *(8 sc)*

Rnd 2: Ch 3, 2 dc in same st, 3 dc in each st around, join in 3rd ch of beg ch-3. *(24 dc)*

Rnd 3: Ch 3, dc in same st, 3 dc in next st, [2 dc in next st, 3 dc in next st] around, join in 3rd ch of beg ch-3. *(60 dc)*

Rnds 4–6: Ch 3, dc in each st around, join in 3rd ch of beg ch-3.

Rnd 7: Ch 3, dc in same st, 2 dc in each st around, join in 3rd ch of beg ch-3. *(120 dc)*

Rnd 8: Rep rnd 4, **turn.**

EDGING

Rnd 1: Holding Front and Back WS tog with Front facing, matching sts, working through both thicknesses, ch 1, sc in each st around, join in beg sc.

Rnd 2: Ch 1, sc in first st, sk next 3 sts, (dc, {ch 1, dc} 3 times) in next st, sk next 3 sts, [sc in next st, sk next 3 sts, (dc, {ch 1, dc} 3 times) in next st, sk next 3 sts] around, join in beg sc, for **hanging lp**, ch 16, sl st in same st as last sl st, **turn**, 23 sc in ch-16 lp, sl st in same st on Pot Holder. Fasten off. ∎

High-Tech Dishcloth

DESIGN BY **JEAN LEINHAUSER**

SKILL LEVEL

EASY

FINISHED SIZE

12¾ inches square

MATERIALS

MEDIUM

- Pisgah Yarn and Dyeing Co., Inc.
  Peaches & Crème medium
  (worsted) weight yarn (2½ oz/
  122 yds/70g per ball):
  1 ball each #89 camel and #121 chocolate
- Size G/6/4mm crochet hook
  or size needed to obtain gauge

GAUGE

4 dc = 1 inch; 2 dc rows = 1 inch

PATTERN NOTES

Chain-3 at beginning of round counts as first
double crochet unless otherwise stated.

Join with slip stitch unless otherwise stated.

INSTRUCTIONS
DISHCLOTH

Rnd 1: With camel, ch 6, **join** *(see Pattern Notes)*
in beg ch to form ring, **ch 3** *(see Pattern Notes)*,
3 dc in ring, ch 3, (4 dc, ch 3) 3 times in ring,
join in 3rd ch of beg ch-3. *(16 dc, 4 ch sps)*

Rnd 2: Working this rnd in **back lps** *(see Stitch
Guide)*, ch 5 *(counts as first dc and ch-2 sp)*, sk
next 2 sts, dc in next st, dc in next ch, *(dc, ch
3, dc) in next ch, dc in next ch, dc in next st,
ch 2, sk next 2 sts, dc in next st, dc in next ch,
rep from * twice, (dc, ch 3, dc) in next ch, dc in
next ch, join in 3rd ch of beg ch-5. Fasten off.

Rnd 3: Join chocolate in first ch of any corner
ch-3 sp, ch 3, *(dc, ch 3, dc) in next ch, dc in

next ch, dc in each of next 3 sts, ch 2, dc in each
of next 3 sts**, dc in next ch, rep from * around,
ending last rep at **, join in 3rd ch of beg ch-3.
Fasten off.

Rnd 4: Join camel in first ch of any corner ch-3
sp, ch 3, *(dc, ch 3, dc) in next ch, dc in next ch,
dc in each of next 5 sts, ch 2, dc in each of next
5 sts**, dc in next ch, rep from * around, ending
last rep at **, join in 3rd ch of beg ch-3.

Rnd 5: Working this rnd in back lps, ch 3, dc in
next st, *dc in next ch, (dc, ch 3, dc) in next ch
sp, dc in next ch, dc in each of next 7 sts, ch 2**,
dc in each of next 7 sts, dc in next ch, rep from *
around, ending last rep at **, dc in each of last
5 sts, join in 3rd ch of beg ch-3. Fasten off.

Rnd 6: Join chocolate in first ch of any corner h-3
sp, ch 3, *(dc, ch 3, dc) in next ch, dc in next ch,
dc in each of next 9 sts, ch 2, dc in each of next 9
sts**, dc in next ch, rep from * around, ending last
rep at **, join in 3rd ch of beg ch-3. Fasten off.

Rnd 7: Join camel in first ch of any corner ch-3
sp, ch 3, *(dc, ch 3, dc) in next ch, dc in next
ch, dc in each of next 11 sts, ch 2, dc in each of
next 11 sts**, dc in next ch, rep from * around,
ending last rep at **, join in 3rd ch of beg ch-3.

Rnd 8: Working this rnd in back lps, ch 3, dc in
next st, *dc in next ch, (dc, ch 3, dc) in next ch
sp, dc in next ch, dc in each of next 13 sts, ch
2**, dc in each of next 13 sts, rep from * around,
ending last rep at **, dc in each of last 11 sts,
join in 3rd ch of beg ch-3. Fasten off.

Rnd 9: Join chocolate in first ch of any corner
ch-3 sp, ch 3, *(dc, ch 3, dc) in next ch, dc in
next ch, dc in each of next 15 sts, ch 2, dc in
each of next 15 sts**, dc in next ch, rep from *
around, ending last rep at **, join in 3rd ch of
beg ch-3. Fasten off.

Rnd 10: Join camel with sc first ch of any corner ch-3 sp, 3 sc in next ch, sc in each ch, sc in each st and sc in each ch-2 sp around with 3 sc in each center corner ch, join in beg sc.

Rnd 11: *Ch 5, sc in 2nd ch from hook, hdc in next ch, dc in next ch, tr in next ch, sk next 3 sts**, sc in next ch, rep from * around, ending last rep at **, join in beg sc. Fasten off. ■

Christmas Tree
Pot Holder

DESIGN BY **ROSETTA HARSHMAN**

SKILL LEVEL

EASY

FINISHED SIZE
9 inches square, hanging lp

MATERIALS
- Medium (worsted) weight cotton yarn:
    - 2½ oz/150 yds/70g white
    - ½ oz/25 yds/14g each green, brown, yellow and red/white/green variegated
- Size I/9/5.5mm crochet hook or size needed to obtain gauge
- Tapestry needle
- Sewing needle
- 1-inch plastic ring
- 4mm beads: 60
- Sewing thread

GAUGE
10 sc = 3 inches; 11 sc rows = 3 inches

PATTERN NOTES
When **changing colors** (see Stitch Guide), always drop unused color to back of work. Do not carry yarn across back of work; use a separate ball of yarn for each color section. Fasten off colors at end of each color section when no longer needed.

Work odd-numbered rows from left to right, work even-numbered rows from right to left.

Each square on chart equals 1 single crochet.

INSTRUCTIONS
FRONT
Row 1: With white, ch 25, sc in 2nd ch from hook, sc in each ch across, turn. (24 sc)

Row 2 (RS): Ch 1, sc in each of first 10 sts, **changing color** (see Pattern Notes) to brown in last st, sc each of next 4 sts, changing to white in last st, sc in each of last 10 sts, turn.

Rows 3–27: Ch 1, sc in each st across, changing colors according to Christmas Tree Chart, turn.

Rnd 28: Now working in rnds, ch 1, 3 sc in first st, sc in each st across with 3 sc in last st, evenly sp 22 sc across ends of rows, working in starting ch on opposite side of row 1, 3 sc in first ch, sc in each ch across with 3 sc in last ch, evenly sp 22 sc across ends of rows, join with sl st in beg sc. Fasten off. (24 sc across each side between corner sc)

Sew beads to tree as desired.

With yellow, using **straight stitch** (see Fig. 1), embroider star to top of tree according to Chart.

Fig. 1
Straight Stitch

BACK
Row 1: With white, ch 25, sc in 2nd ch from hook, sc in each ch across, turn. (24 sc)

Rows 2–27: Ch 1, sc in each st across, turn.

Rnd 28: Rep rnd 28 of Front.

BORDER

Rnd 1: Holding Front and Back WS tog with Front facing, matching sts, working through both thicknesses, join variegated with sc in any center corner st, 2 sc in same st, sc in each st around with 3 sc in each center corner st, join with sl st in beg sc. *(26 sc across each side between corner sc)*

Rnd 2: Ch 1, (sc, ch 1, sc) in first st, sk next st, *(sc, ch 1, sc) in next st, sk next st, rep from * around, join with sl st in beg sc. Fasten off.

For **hanging lp**, join variegated with **sc in plastic ring** *(see Fig. 2)*, work 22 sc in ring, join with sl st in beg sc. Fasten off, leaving long strand for sewing.

Sew hanging lp to last rnd of Border as shown in photo. ■

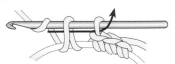

Fig. 2
Single Crochet Over Ring

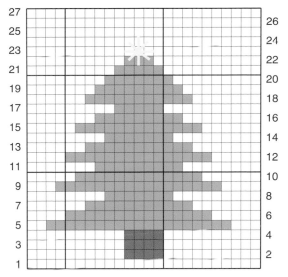

Christmas Tree Chart

COLOR KEY
■ Brown
■ Green
☐ White
Yellow straight stitch

Daisy Scrubbie

DESIGN BY **DENISE ROTHBERG**

SKILL LEVEL

INTERMEDIATE

FINISHED SIZE
7½ inches across

MATERIALS
- Medium (worsted) weight cotton yarn:
    1 oz/50 yds/28g each white and yellow
- Size G/6/4mm crochet hook
- Plastic mesh pot scrubber

PATTERN NOTE
Join with slip stitch as indicated unless otherwise stated.

INSTRUCTIONS

SCRUBBIE

Rnd 1: With yellow, place sl st on hook, working around outer edge of plastic scrubber, insert hook in any lp, yo, pull lp through, yo, pull through 2 lps on hook (*sc made*), evenly sp 39 more sc around, **join** (*see Pattern Note*) in beg sc. (*40 sc*)

Rnd 2: Ch 1, sc in first st, 2 sc in next st, [sc in next st, 2 sc in next st] around, join in beg sc. (*60 sc*)

Rnd 3: Join white in first st, [ch 7, sc in 2nd ch from hook, hdc in each of last 5 chs, sl st in each of next 2 sts on last rnd] 29 times, ch 7, sc in 2nd ch from hook, hdc in each of last 5 chs, sl st in last st, join in beg sl st.

Rnd 4: Ch 1, working on opposite side of ch on first ch-7, sc in each of first 6 chs, ch 3, sc in each of next 6 sts, [sl st in next sl st, working on opposite side of next ch-7, sc in each of first 6 chs, ch 3, sc in each of next 6 sts] 29 times, sl st in last sl st, join in beg sc. Fasten off. ■

Sunflower **Scrubbie**

DESIGN BY **DENISE ROTHBERG**

SKILL LEVEL

EASY

FINISHED SIZE

7½ inches across

MATERIALS

- Medium (worsted) weight cotton yarn:
  1 oz/50 yds/28g each gold and brown
- Size G/6/4mm crochet hook
- Plastic mesh pot scrubber

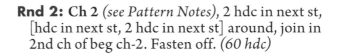

MEDIUM

PATTERN NOTES

Join with slip stitch as indicated unless otherwise stated

Chain-2 at beginning of round counts as first half double crochet unless otherwise stated.

INSTRUCTIONS
SCRUBBIE

Rnd 1: With brown, place sl st on hook, working around outer edge of plastic scrubber, insert hook in any lp, yo, pull lp through, yo, pull through 2 lps on hook *(sc made)*, evenly sp 39 more sc around, **join** *(see Pattern Notes)* in beg sc. *(40 sc)*

Rnd 2: Ch 2 *(see Pattern Notes)*, 2 hdc in next st, [hdc in next st, 2 hdc in next st] around, join in 2nd ch of beg ch-2. Fasten off. *(60 hdc)*

Rnd 3: Join gold in first st, (ch 2, dc, 3 tr, dc, hdc) in same st, sk next st, sc in next st, *(hdc, dc, 3 tr, dc, hdc) in next st, sk next st, sc in next st, rep from * around, join in 2nd ch of beg ch-2.

Rnd 4: Ch 1, sc in each of first 3 sts, (sc, ch 3, sc) in next st, sc in each of next 3 sts, sl st in next st, [sc in each of next 3 sts, (sc, ch 3, sc) in next st, sc in each of next 3 sts, sl st in next st] around, join in beg sc. Fasten off. ∎

Stars & Stripes
Pot Holder
DESIGN BY **DIANE POELLOT**

SKILL LEVEL

EASY

FINISHED SIZE
9¼ inch square, not including hanging lp

MATERIALS
- Pisgah Yarn and Dyeing Co., Inc. Peaches & Crème medium (worsted) weight yarn (2½ oz/ 122 yds/70g per ball):
  - 1 ball each #1 white, #95 red and #9 bright navy
- Size H/8/5mm crochet hook or size needed to obtain gauge

4 MEDIUM

GAUGE
7 sc = 2 inches; 7 sc rows = 2 inches

PATTERN NOTES
When **changing colors** (*see Stitch Guide*), always drop unused color to back side of work. Work over dropped color and carry across to next section of same color. Fasten off each color when no longer needed.

Work odd-numbered rows from left to right, work even-numbered rows from right to left.

Each square on chart equals 1 single crochet.

INSTRUCTIONS
FRONT
Row 1: With white, ch 28, sc in 2nd ch from hook and in each ch across, turn. (*27 sc*)

Row 2 (RS): Ch 1, sc in each of first 13 sts, **changing color** (*see Pattern Notes*) to red in last st, sc in next st, changing to white, sc in each of last 13 sts, turn.

Rows 3–26: Ch 1, sc in each st across changing colors according to Heart Chart, turn. Fasten off at end of last row.

Rnd 27: Now working in rnds around outer edge, with RS facing, join bright navy with sc in any st, sc in each st and in end of each row around with 3 sc in each corner, join with sl st in beg sc. Fasten off.

Rnd 28: Join white with sc in any st, sc in each st around with 3 sc in each center corner st, join with sl st in beg sc. Fasten off.

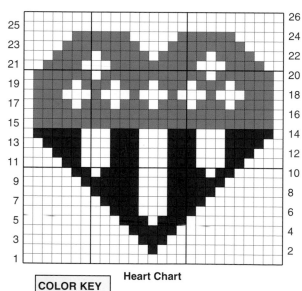

Heart Chart

COLOR KEY
☐ White
■ Red
■ Bright Navy

BACK

Row 1: With white, ch 28, sc in 2nd ch from hook and in each ch across, turn. *(27 sc)*

Rows 2–26: Ch 1, sc in each st across, turn.

Rnds 27 & 28: Rep rnds 27 and 28 of Front.

Rnd 29: Holding Front and Back WS tog with Front facing, matching sts, working through both thicknesses, join red with sc in center corner st at upper right-hand corner, sc in each st around with 3 sc in each center corner st, 2 sc in same st as beg sc, for **hanging lp**, ch 8, sl st in top of last st made to form ring, 23 sc in ring. Fasten off. ■

Granny Square

DESIGN BY KATHERINE ENG

SKILL LEVEL

EASY

FINISHED SIZE
10 inches square

MATERIALS
- Pisgah Yarn and Dyeing Co., Inc. Peaches & Crème medium (worsted) weight yarn (2½ oz/ 122 yds/70g per ball): 1 ball each #1 white, #26 light blue and #28 delft blue
- Size F/5/3.75mm crochet hook or size needed to obtain gauge
- Tapestry needle

GAUGE
Block = 2¾ inches square

PATTERN NOTES
Join with slip stitch as indicated unless otherwise stated.

Chain-3 at beginning of round counts as first double crochet unless otherwise stated.

INSTRUCTIONS
BLOCK
MAKE 9.
Rnd 1: With delft blue, ch 4, **join** (see Pattern Notes) in beg ch to form ring, **ch 3** (see Pattern Notes), 2 dc in ring, ch 2, (3 dc in ring, ch 2) 3 times, join in 3rd ch of beg ch-3. Fasten off. (12 dc, 4 ch sps)

Rnd 2: Join white in any corner ch sp, (ch 3, 2 dc, ch 2, 3 dc) in same sp, ch 1, *(3 dc, ch 2, 3 dc) in next ch sp, ch 1, rep from * around, join in 3rd ch of beg ch-3. Fasten off.

Rnd 3: Join light blue with sc in any corner ch sp, (sc, ch 3, 2 sc) in same sp, *ch 1, sk next st, sc in next st, ch 1, sk next st, 2 sc in next ch-1 sp, ch 1, sk next st, sc in next st, ch 1, sk next st**, (2 sc, ch 3, 2 sc) in next corner ch sp, rep from * around ending last rep at **, join in beg sc. Fasten off.

Separate a strand of light blue into 2-ply lengths.

Hold Blocks WS tog, matching sts, with 2-ply strand, sew tog through **back lps** (see Stitch Guide) in 3 rows of 3 blocks each.

BORDER
Rnd 1: Join light blue with sc in any corner ch sp, (ch 3, sc) in same sp, *[ch 2, sc in next ch sp, ch 1, sc in next ch sp, ch 2, sc in next ch sp, ch 1, sc in next ch sp, ch 2, sc in next ch sp before next seam, ch 1, sc in next ch sp after same seam] twice, [ch 2, sc in next ch sp, ch 1, sc in next ch sp] twice, ch 2**, (sc, ch 3, sc) in next corner ch sp, rep from * around ending last rep at **, join in beg sc. Fasten off.

Rnd 2: Join white with sc in any corner ch sp, (ch 3, sc) in same sp, *sc in next st, [ch 2, sc in next st, ch 1, sc in next st] 8 times, ch 2, sc in next st**, (sc, ch 3, sc) in next corner ch sp, rep from * around, ending last rep at **, join in beg sc. Fasten off.

Rnd 3: Join delft blue in any corner ch sp, (ch 3, sl st, ch 4, sl st, ch 3, sl st) in same sp, *ch 2, (sl st, ch 3, sl st) in next ch-2 sp, [ch 2, sl st in next ch-1 sp, ch 2, (sl st, ch 3, sl st) in next ch-2 sp] across to next corner ch sp**, (sl st, ch 3, sl st, ch 4, sl st, ch 3, sl st) in next corner ch sp, rep from * around, ending last rep at **, join in beg sl st. Fasten off. ∎

Circle **Pot Holder** DESIGN BY **JOAN DROST**

SKILL LEVEL
■■□□
EASY

FINISHED SIZE
6½ inches in diameter

MATERIALS
- Pisgah Yarn and Dyeing Co., Inc. Peaches & Crème medium (worsted) weight yarn (2½ oz/ 122 yds/70g per ball): 1 ball each #33 persimmon, #51 apple green and #49 deep purple
- Size G/6/4mm crochet hook or size needed to obtain gauge

GAUGE
4 sc = 1 inch; 4 sc rows = 1 inch

PATTERN NOTES
Join with slip stitch as indicated unless otherwise stated

Chain-3 at beginning of round counts as first double crochet unless otherwise stated.

INSTRUCTIONS
FRONT
Rnd 1: With apple green, ch 5, **join** (see Pattern Notes) in beg ch to form ring, ch 1, 12 sc in ring, join in beg sc. Fasten off. (12 sc)

Rnd 2: Join deep purple with sc in first st, 2 sc in next st, [sc in next st, 2 sc in next st] around, join in beg sc. Fasten off. (18 sc)

Rnd 3: Join persimmon in first st, **ch 3** (see Pattern Notes), dc in each of next 2 sts, ch 2, [dc in each of next 3 sts, ch 2] around, join in 3rd ch of beg ch-3. (18 dc, 6 ch sps)

Rnd 4: Ch 3, dc in same st, dc in next st, 2 dc in next st, ch 2, sk next ch sp, [2 dc in next st, dc in next st, 2 dc in next st, ch 2, sk next ch sp] around, join in 3rd ch of beg ch-3. (30 dc, 6 ch sps)

Rnd 5: Ch 3, tr in same st, dc in next st, hdc in next st, dc in next st, (tr, ch 3, sl st) in next st, sl st in next ch sp, [sl st in next st, ch 3, tr in same st, dc in next st, hdc in next st, dc in next st, (tr, ch 3, sl st) in next st, sl st in next ch sp] around, join in first ch of beg ch-3. Fasten off.

Rnd 6: Join deep purple with sc in first ch of first ch-3, sc in each of next 2 chs, sc in each of next 5 sts, sc in each of next 3 chs of next ch-3, working over sl st, sc in next ch-2 sp on rnd 4, [sc in each of next 3 chs of next ch-3, sc in each of next 5 sts, sc in each of next 3 chs of next ch-3, working over sl st, sc in next ch-2 sp on rnd 4] around, join in beg sc. Fasten off. (72 sc)

Rnd 7: Join apple green in first st, ch 2 (counts as first hdc), sk next st, sc in each of next 8 sts, sk next st, [hdc in each of next 2 sts, sk next st, sc in each of next 8 sts, sk next st] around to last st, hdc in last st, join in 2nd ch of beg ch-2. Fasten off. (60 sts)

BACK
Rnd 1: With deep purple, ch 4, join in beg ch to form ring, ch 3, 11 dc in ring, join in 3rd ch of beg ch-3. (12 dc)

Rnd 2: Ch 3, dc in same st, 2 dc in each st around, join in 3rd ch of beg ch-3. (24 dc)

Rnd 3: Ch 3, 2 dc in next st, [dc in next st, 2 dc in next st] around, join in 3rd ch of beg ch-3. (36 dc)

Rnd 4: Ch 3, dc in next st, 2 dc in next st, [dc in each of next 2 sts, 2 dc in next st] around, join in 3rd ch of beg ch-3. (48 dc)

Rnd 5: Ch 3, dc in each of next 2 sts, 2 dc in next st, [dc in each of next 3 sts, 2 dc in next st] around, join in 3rd ch of beg ch-3. (60 dc)

Rnd 6: Holding Front and Back WS tog, matching sts, working through both thicknesses in **back lps** (see Stitch Guide), ch 1, sc in each st around, for **hanging lp**, ch 8, join in beg sc. Fasten off. ■

Flying Squares
Hot Pad

DESIGN BY ROSE PIRRONE

SKILL LEVEL

EASY

FINISHED SIZE
10½ inches square

MATERIALS
- Medium (worsted) weight cotton yarn:
  2½ oz/150 yds/70g each blue and gold
- Size G/6/4mm crochet hook or size needed to obtain gauge

GAUGE
Rnds 1–7 = 4 inches square

SPECIAL STITCH
Puff stitch (puff st): Working over next ch sp on last rnd, [yo, insert hook in next ch sp on rnd before last, yo, pull up ⅜-inch lp, [working over ch sp on last rnd, yo, insert hook in same ch sp on rnd before last, yo, pull lp through] twice, yo, pull through all 7 lps on hook.

INSTRUCTIONS
HOT PAD
Rnd 1: With blue, ch 4, 2 dc in 4th ch from hook (*first 3 chs count as first dc*), ch 1, (3 dc, ch 1) 3 times in same ch, drop blue, insert hook in 3rd ch of beg ch-3, pull gold through ch and lp on hook. (*12 dc, 4 ch sps*)

Rnd 2: Ch 1, sc in each of first 3 sts, ch 2, sk next ch sp, [sc in each of next 3 sts, ch 2, sk next ch sp] around, drop gold, insert hook in beg sc, pull blue through st and lp on hook.

Rnd 3: Ch 1, sc in each of first 3 sts, (**puff st**—*see Special Stitch*, ch 2, puff st) in next ch sp on rnd before last, *sc in each of next 3 sts, (puff st, ch 2, puff st) in next ch sp on rnd before last, rep from * around, drop blue, insert hook in beg sc, pull gold through st and lp on hook.

Rnd 4: Ch 1, 2 sc in first st, sc in each sc across to next puff st, sc in next puff st, (puff st, ch 2, puff st) in next ch sp on rnd before last, sk next puff st, *2 sc in next sc, sc in each sc across to next puff st, sc in next puff st, (puff st, ch 2, puff st) in next ch sp on rnd before last, sk next puff st, rep from * around, drop gold, insert hook in beg sc, pull blue through st and lp on hook.

Rnd 5: Rep rnd 4, changing to gold.

Rnds 6–17: [Rep rnds 4 and 5 alternately] 6 times.

Rnd 18: Rep rnd 4.

Rnd 19: Ch 1, [sc in each sc and in each puff st around to next ch sp, working over next ch sp on last rnd, 3 sc in next ch sp on rnd before last] around, drop blue, insert hook in beg sc, pull gold through st and lp on hook.

Rnd 20: Ch 1, sc in first st, ch 3, [sc in next st, ch 3] around, join with sl st in beg sc. Fasten off. ■

Shaded Pastel
Dishcloth

DESIGN BY **JO ANN LOFTIS**

SKILL LEVEL

EASY

FINISHED SIZE
9½ inches in diameter, not including hanger

MATERIALS
- Pisgah Yarn and Dyeing Co., Inc. Peaches & Crème medium (worsted) weight yarn (2 oz/ 98 yds/56g per ball):
  1 ball #130 shaded pastels
- Size G/6/4mm crochet hook or size needed to obtain gauge

GAUGE
Rnds 1 and 2 = 3 inches across

PATTERN NOTES
Join with slip stitch as indicated unless otherwise stated.

Chain-3 at beginning of round counts as first double crochet unless otherwise stated.

SPECIAL STITCHES
Beginning cluster (beg cl): Ch 3, yo, insert hook in designated st, yo, pull lp through, yo, pull through 2 lps on hook, yo, insert hook in same st, yo, pull lp through, yo, pull through 2 lps on hook, yo, pull through all 3 lps on hook.

Cluster (cl): Yo, insert hook in designated st, yo, pull lp through, yo, pull through 2 lps on hook, [yo, insert hook in same st, yo, pull lp through, yo, pull through 2 lps on hook] twice, yo, pull through all 4 lps on hook.

INSTRUCTIONS
DISHCLOTH

Rnd 1: Ch 4, **join** (see Pattern Notes) in beg ch to form ring, **ch 3** (see Pattern Notes), 11 dc in ring, join in 3rd ch of beg ch-3. (12 dc)

Rnd 2: Ch 3, dc in same st, 2 dc in each st around, join in 3rd ch of beg ch-3. (24 dc)

Rnd 3: **Beg cl** (see Special Stitches) in first st, ch 3, sk next st, [**cl** (see Special Stitches) in next st, ch 3, sk next st] around, join in top of beg cl.

Rnd 4: Ch 3, dc in first ch of next ch-3, 2 dc in same sp, [dc in next cl, dc in first ch of next ch-3, 2 dc in same ch sp] around, join in 3rd ch of beg ch-3.

Rnd 5: Beg cl in first st, ch 3, sk next st, [cl in next st, ch 3, sk next st] around, join in top of beg cl.

Rnd 6: Ch 1, sc in first st, sc in first ch of next ch-3, 2 sc in same sp, [sc in next cl, sc in first ch of next ch-3, 2 sc in same ch sp] around, join in beg sc.

Rnd 7: Ch 1, sk next 3 sts, *(dc, {ch 1, dc} 4 times) in next st, sk next 3 sts, sc in next st, sk next 3 sts, rep from * 10 times, (dc, {ch 1, dc} 4 times) in next st, sk next 3 sts, join in joining sl st of last rnd, for **hanger**, ch 10, sl st in same st as last sl st. Fasten off. ∎

FIESTA

DESIGN BY **DEBORAH LEVI-HAMBURG**

SKILL LEVEL

EASY

FINISHED SIZE
11 inches in diameter

MATERIALS
- Pisgah Yarn and Dyeing Co., Inc. Peaches & Crème medium (worsted) weight yarn (2½ oz/ 122 yds/70g per ball):
  1 ball each #12 gold, #46 rose pink, #19 peacock, #49 deep purple and #33 persimmon
- Size G/6/4mm crochet hook or size needed to obtain gauge
- Stitch marker

GAUGE
Rnds 1–4 = 2¼ inches across

PATTERN NOTE
Do not join or turn rounds unless otherwise stated. Mark first stitch of each round.

INSTRUCTIONS
POT HOLDER
Rnd 1: With gold, ch 6, sl st in beg ch to form ring, ch 1, 9 sc in ring. *(9 sc)*

Rnd 2: 2 sc in each st around. *(18 sc)*

Rnd 3: [Sc in next st, 2 sc in next st] around. *(27 sc)*

Rnd 4: Sc in each st around.

Rnd 5: [Sc in each of next 2 sts, 2 sc in next st] around. *(36 sc)*

Rnd 6: Sc in each st around.

Rnd 7: [Sc in each of next 3 sts, 2 sc in next st] around. *(45 sc)*

Rnd 8: Sc in each st around.

Rnd 9: [Sc in each of next 4 sts, 2 sc in next st] around. *(54 sc)*

Rnd 10: Sc in each st around.

Rnd 11: [Sc in each of next 5 sts, 2 sc in next st] around. *(63 sc)*

Rnd 12: [Sc in each of next 8 sts, 2 sc in n ext st] around, join with sl st in beg sc. Fasten off. *(70 sc)*

Rnd 13: Join rose pink with sc in any st, tr in next st *(push tr to front)*, [sc in next st, tr in next st] around, join with sl st in beg sc. Fasten off. *(35 sc, 35 tr)*

Rnd 14: Join gold with sc in any st, *[sc in each of next 2 sts, 2 sc in next st] 3 times, [sc in each of next 4 sts, 2 sc in next st] 5 times, rep from *, sc in last st, join with sl st in beg sc. Fasten off. *(86 sc)*

Rnd 15: Join peacock with sc in any st, tr in next st, [sc in next st, tr in next st] around, join with sl st in beg sc. Fasten off. *(43 sc, 43 tr)*

Rnd 16: Join gold with sc in any st, sc in next st, 2 sc in next st, sc in each of next 2 sts, 2 sc in next st, [sc in each of next 7 sts, 2 sc in next st] around, join with sl st in beg sc. Fasten off. *(98 sc)*

Rnd 17: Join deep purple with sc in any st, tr in next st, [sc in next st, tr in next st] around, join with sl st in beg sc. Fasten off. *(49 sc, 49 tr)*

Rnd 18: Join gold with sc in any st, sc in each of next 5 sts, 2 sc in next st, [sc in each of next 6 sts, 2 sc in next st] around, join with sl st in beg sc. Fasten off. *(112 sc)*

Rnd 19: Join persimmon with sc in any st, tr in next st, [sc in next st, tr in next st] around, join with sl st in beg sc. Fasten off. *(56 sc, 56 tr)*

Rnd 20: Join gold with sc in any st, sc in each of next 6 sts, 2 sc in next st, [sc in each of next 7 sts, 2 sc in next st] around, join with sl st in beg sc. *(126 sc)*

Rnd 21: Ch 1, sc in first st, tr in next st, [sc in next st, tr in next st] around, join with sl st in beg sc. Fasten off. *(63 sc, 63 tr)* ∎

Yellow Popcorn
Pot Holder

DESIGN BY **JUDY TEAGUE TREECE**

SKILL LEVEL

EASY

FINISHED SIZE
8 inches across, not including hanging lp

MATERIALS
- Size 3 crochet cotton:
  70 yds each yellow and blue
  25 yds white
- Size F/5/3.75mm crochet hook
  or size needed to obtain gauge

GAUGE
9 dc = 2 inches; 5 dc rows = 2 inches

PATTERN NOTES
Join with slip stitch as indicated unless
otherwise stated.

Chain-3 at beginning of round counts as first
double crochet unless otherwise stated.

SPECIAL STITCHES
Beginning popcorn (beg pc): Ch 3, 4 dc in same st,
drop lp from hook, insert hook in 3rd ch of beg
ch-3, pull dropped lp through.

Popcorn (pc): 5 dc in next st, drop lp from hook,
insert hook in first st of 5-dc group, pull
dropped lp through.

INSTRUCTIONS
FRONT
Rnd 1: With yellow, ch 4, 11 dc in 4th ch from
hook (*first 3 chs count as first dc*), **join** (*see
Pattern Notes*) in 3rd ch of beg ch-3. (*12 dc*)

Rnd 2: **Beg pc** (*see Special Stitches*) in first st,
3 dc in next st, [**pc** (*see Special Stitches*) in next

st, 3 dc in next st] around, join in top of beg pc.
(*18 dc, 6 pc*)

Rnd 3: **Ch 3** (*see Pattern Notes*), pc in next st,
3 dc in next st, pc in next st, [dc in next st, pc
in next st, 3 dc in next st, pc in next st] around,
join in 3rd ch of beg ch-3. (*24 dc, 12 pc*)

Rnd 4: Ch 3, dc in next st, pc in next st, 3 dc in
next st, pc in next st, [dc in each of next 3 sts, pc
in next st, 3 dc in next st, pc in next st] around
to last st, dc in last st, join in 3rd ch of beg ch-3.
(*36 dc, 12 pc*)

Rnd 5: Ch 3, *pc in next st, dc in each of next
2 sts, 3 dc in next st, dc in each of next 2 sts, pc
in next st**, dc in next st, rep from * around,
ending last rep at **, join in 3rd ch of beg ch-3.
(*48 dc, 12 pc*)

Rnd 6: Beg pc in first st, dc in each of next 4 sts,
3 dc in next st, dc in each of next 4 sts, [pc in
next st, dc in each of next 4 sts, 3 dc in next st,
dc in each of next 4 sts] around, join in top of
beg pc. (*66 dc, 6 pc*)

Rnd 7: Ch 3, dc in each of next 5 sts, 3 dc in next
st, [dc in each of next 11 sts, 3 dc in next st]
5 times, dc in each of last 5 sts, join in 3rd ch
of beg ch-3. Fasten off. (*84 dc*)

Rnd 8: Join white in first st, ch 3, dc in each
of next 6 sts, 3 dc in next st, [dc in each of
next 13 sts, 3 dc in next st] 5 times, dc in each
of last 6 sts, join in 3rd ch of beg ch-3. Fasten
off. (*96 dc*)

Rnd 9: Join blue in first st, ch 3, dc in each of
next 7 sts, 3 dc in next st, [dc in each of next
15 sts, 3 dc in next st] 5 times, dc in each of
last 7 sts, join in 3rd ch of beg ch-3. Fasten
off. (*108 dc*)

BACK

Rnd 1: With blue, ch 4, 11 dc in 4th ch from hook *(first 3 chs count as first dc)*, join in top of beg ch-3. *(12 dc)*

Rnd 2: Ch 3, 3 dc in next st, [dc in next st, 3 dc in next st] around, join in 3rd ch of beg ch-3. *(24 dc)*

Rnds 3–9: Ch 3, dc in each st around with 3 dc in center st of each 3-dc group, join in 3rd ch of beg ch-3. Fasten off at end of last rnd. *(108 dc at end of last rnd)*

BORDER

Rnd 1: Holding Front and Back WS tog with Front facing, matching sts, working through both thicknesses, join white with sc in center st of any 3-dc group, sc in same st, sc in each st around with 3 sc in center st of each 3-dc group, sc in same st as first sc, join in beg sc. *(120 sc)*

Rnd 2: Ch 1, sc in each of first 2 sts, **turn**, for **hanging lp**, (sl st, ch 10, sl st) in next st, **turn**, ch 1, 20 sc in ch sp just made, sl st in next st, [sc in next st, ch 3, sk next st] 9 times, (sc, ch 3, sc) in next st, *ch 3, sk next st, [sc in next st, ch 3, sk next st] 9 times, (sc, ch 3, sc) in next st, rep from * 3 times, [ch 3, sk next st, sc in next st] 9 times, sc in last st, join in beg sc. Fasten off. ∎

Mum Dishcloth

DESIGN BY **SHERI L. JACOBSON**

SKILL LEVEL

EASY

FINISHED SIZE
11½ inches in diameter

MATERIALS
- Pisgah Yarn and Dyeing Co., Inc. Peaches & Crème medium (worsted) weight yarn (2½ oz/ 122 yds/70g per ball):
  1 ball each #51 apple green, #31 shocking pink and #12 gold
- Size G/6/4mm crochet hook or size needed to obtain gauge

GAUGE
Rnds 1–4 = 2½ inches across

PATTERN NOTES
Join with slip stitch as indicated unless otherwise stated.

Chain-3 at beginning of round counts as first double crochet unless otherwise stated.

INSTRUCTIONS
DISHCLOTH
Rnd 1: With gold, ch 3, **join** (see Pattern Notes) in beg ch to form ring, ch 1, 7 sc in ring, join in beg sc. (7 sc)

Rnd 2: For **petals**, ch 3, sl st in 2nd ch from hook, sl st in next ch, [sl st in **front lp** (see Stitch Guide) of next st in ring, ch 3, sl st in 2nd ch from hook, sl st in next ch] around, join in joining sl st of last rnd. Fasten off. (7 petals)

Rnd 3: Working this rnd in **back lps** (see Stitch Guide) of rnd 1, join shocking pink with sc in any st, sc in same st, 2 sc in each st around, join in beg sc. (14 sc)

Rnd 4: For **petals**, ch 1, sc in front lp of first st, [ch 4, sl st in 2nd ch from hook, sl st in each of next 2 chs, sc in front lp of next st on last rnd] around, ch 4, sl st in 2nd ch from hook, sl st in each of next 2 chs, join in beg sc. Fasten off. (14 petals)

Rnd 5: Working this rnd in back lps of rnd 3, join shocking pink with sc in any st, 2 sc in next st, [sc in next st, 2 sc in next st] around, join in beg sc. (21 sc)

Rnd 6: Rep rnd 4. (21 petals)

Rnd 7: Working this rnd in back lps of rnd 5, join shocking pink with sc in any st, sc in next st, 2 sc in next st, [sc in each of next 2 sts, 2 sc in next st] around, join in beg sc. (28 sc)

Rnd 8: Rep rnd 4. (28 petals)

Rnd 9: Working this rnd in back lps of rnd 7, join shocking pink in any st, **ch 3** (see Pattern Notes), dc in same st, dc in next st, [2 dc in next st, dc in next st] around, join in 3rd ch of beg ch-3. Fasten off. (42 dc)

Rnd 10: Join apple green with sc in any st, sc in each of next 5 sts, 2 sc in next st, [sc in each of next 6 sts, 2 sc in next st] around, join in beg sc. (48 sc)

Rnd 11: Ch 3, dc in same st, dc in each of next 2 sts, [ch 1, dc in each of next 7 sts] 6 times, ch 1, dc in each of last 3 sts, join in 3rd ch of beg ch-3. *(49 dc, 7 ch sps)*

Rnd 12: Ch 3, dc in next st, *dc dec *(see Stitch Guide)* in next 2 sts, ch 3, dc in next ch-1 sp, ch 3, dc dec in next 2 sts**, dc in each of next 3 sts, rep from * around, ending last rep at **, dc in last st, join in 3rd ch of beg ch-3. *(42 dc, 14 ch sps)*

Rnd 13: Ch 3, *dc dec in next 2 sts, ch 3, sk next ch sp, 5 dc in next dc, ch 3, sk next ch sp, dc dec in next 2 sts**, dc in next st, rep from * around ending last rep at **, join in 3rd ch of beg ch-3. *(56 dc, 14 ch sps)*

Rnd 14: Sl st in next st, sl st in each of next 3 chs, sl st in next dc, ch 3, 2 dc in same st, *dc in each of next 3 sts, 3 dc in next st, ch 3, sk next ch sp, dc dec in next 3 sts, ch 3, sk next ch sp**, 3 dc in next st, rep from * around, ending last rep at **, join in 3rd ch of beg ch-3.

Rnd 15: Ch 3, 2 dc in same st, *dc in each of next 7 sts, 3 dc in next st, ch 2, sk next ch sp, sc in next st, ch 2, sk next ch sp**, 3 dc in next st, rep from * around, ending last rep at **, join in 3rd ch of beg ch-3.

Rnd 16: Ch 3, 5 dc in same st, *sk next 2 sts, sc in next st, ch 2, sk next 2 sts, (dc, ch 2, dc) in next st, ch 2, sk next 2 sts, sc in next st, sk next 2 sts, 6 dc in next st, sk next 2 ch sps**, 6 dc in next st, rep from * around, ending last rep at **, join in 3rd ch of beg ch-3. Fasten off. ∎

Mum Scrubbie

DESIGN BY **SHERI L. JACOBSON**

SKILL LEVEL

EASY

FINISHED SIZE
3¾ inches in diameter, not including hanger

MATERIALS
- Pisgah Yarn and Dyeing Co., Inc. Peaches & Crème medium (worsted) weight yarn (2½ oz/ 122 yds/70g per ball): 1 ball each #51 apple green, #31 shocking pink and #12 gold
- Size G/6/4mm crochet hook or size needed to obtain gauge
- Tapestry needle
- 1-inch plastic ring
- Plastic mesh pot scrubber
- Safety pins

GAUGE
Rnds 1–4 = 2½ inches across

PATTERN NOTES
Join with slip stitch as indicated unless otherwise stated.

Chain-3 at beginning of round counts as first double crochet unless otherwise stated.

INSTRUCTIONS
SCRUBBIE
Rnd 1: With gold, ch 3, **join** *(see Pattern Notes)* in beg ch to form ring, ch 1, 7 sc in ring, join in beg sc. *(7 sc)*

Rnd 2: For **petals**, ch 3, sl st in 2nd ch from hook, sl st in next ch, [sl st in **front lp** *(see Stitch Guide)* of next st in ring, ch 3, sl st in 2nd ch from hook, sl st in next ch] around, join in joining sl st of last rnd. Fasten off. *(7 petals)*

Rnd 3: Working this rnd in **back lps** *(see Stitch Guide)* of rnd 1, join shocking pink with sc in any st, sc in same st, 2 sc in each st around, join in beg sc. *(14 sc)*

Rnd 4: For **petals**, ch 1, sc in front lp of first st, [ch 4, sl st in 2nd ch from hook, sl st in each of next 2 chs, sc in front lp of next st on last rnd] around, ch 4, sl st in 2nd ch from hook, sl st in each of next 2 chs, join in beg sc. Fasten off. *(14 petals)*

Rnd 5: Working this rnd in back lps of rnd 3, join shocking pink with sc in any st, 2 sc in next st, [sc in next st, 2 sc in next st] around, join in beg sc. *(21 sc)*

Rnd 6: Rep rnd 4. *(21 petals)*

Rnd 7: Working this rnd in back lps of rnd 5, join shocking pink with sc in any st, sc in next st, 2 sc in next st, [sc in each of next 2 sts, 2 sc in next st] around, join in beg sc. *(28 sc)*

Rnd 8: Rep rnd 4. *(28 petals)*

Rnd 9: Working this rnd in back lps of rnd 7, join shocking pink in any st, **ch 3** *(see Pattern Notes)*, dc in same st, dc in next st, [2 dc in next st, dc in next st] around, join in 3rd ch of beg ch-3. Fasten off. *(42 dc)*

Note: Using safety pins, pin rnd 9 to outer edge of plastic scrubber. Remove pins when needed as you work.

Rnd 10: Ch 1, insert hook in first st and under 5 or 6 plastic mesh strands, yo, pull lp through, complete as sc, sp sts evenly around scrubber, [insert hook in next st and under 5 or 6 plastic mesh strands, yo, pull lp through, complete as sc] around, join in beg sc. Fasten off.

LEAF
MAKE 2.
With apple green, ch 11, tr in 4th ch from hook, 2 tr in next ch, dc in next ch, hdc in next ch, 2 dc in next ch, dc in next ch, hdc in next ch, (sc, ch 3, sl st in 2nd ch from hook, ch 1, sc) in last ch, working on opposite side of ch, hdc in next ch, dc in next ch, 2 dc in next ch, hdc in next ch, dc in next ch, 2 tr in next ch, tr in next ch, dc in last ch. Fasten off, leaving long strand for sewing.

Sew Leaves side by side to last rnd of Scrubbie.

HANGER
Join apple green with **sc in plastic ring** *(see Fig. 1)*, 19 sc in ring, join in beg sc. Fasten off, leaving long strand for sewing.

Sew to last rnd of Scrubbie opposite Leaves. ∎

Fig. 1
Single Crochet Over Ring

Daisy Pot Holder

DESIGN BY **ELIZABETH WHITE**

SKILL LEVEL

EASY

FINISHED SIZE
8 inches square, not including hanger

MATERIALS
- Pisgah Yarn and Dyeing Co., Inc. America's Best size 10 crochet cotton (150 yds per ball): 1 ball each #5 queens lace and #28 denim
- Size 5/1.90mm steel crochet hook or size needed to obtain gauge
- Tapestry needle

GAUGE
7 dc and 1 ch-1 sp = 1 inch; 7 dc rows = 2 inches

PATTERN NOTE
Chain-4 at beginning of row counts as first double crochet and chain-1 space unless otherwise stated.

INSTRUCTIONS
SIDE
MAKE 2.
Row 1: With denim, ch 63, dc in 7th ch from hook (*first 4 chs count as first dc and ch-1 sp*), [ch 1, sk next ch, dc in next ch] across, turn. (*30 dc, 29 ch sps*)

Row 2: **Ch 4** (*see Pattern Note*), sk next ch sp, dc in next st, [dc in next ch sp, dc in next st] 3 times, *ch 1, sk next ch sp, dc in next st, [dc in next ch sp, dc in next st] 3 times, rep from * across to last ch sp, ch 1, sk next ch sp, dc in last st, turn. (*51 dc, 8 ch sps*)

Row 3: Ch 4, sk next ch sp, [dc in each of next 3 sts, ch 1, sk next st, dc in each of next 3 sts, ch 1, sk next ch sp] across to last st, dc in last st, turn.

Row 4: Ch 4, sk next ch sp, [dc in each of next 3 sts, dc in next ch sp, dc in each of next 3 sts, ch 1, sk next ch sp] across to last st, dc in last st, turn.

Row 5: Ch 4, sk next ch sp, dc in next st, [ch 1, sk next st or ch sp, dc in next st] across, turn.

Rows 6–29: [Rep rows 2–5 consecutively] 6 times. Fasten off at end of last row.

For **front**, with 3 strands queens lace held tog, using **straight stitch** (*see Fig. 1*), starting at top left corner, embroider every other square according to embroidery diagram around outer edge of 1 Side (*see photo*).

EDGING
Holding Sides WS tog with front facing, matching sts, working through both thicknesses, join queens lace with sl st in any corner ch sp, for **hanger**, ch 15, (sc, ch 2, 2 dc) in same sp, (sc, ch 2, 2 dc) in each ch sp and in each row around with (sc, ch 2, 2 dc) twice in each corner ch sp, (sc, ch 2, 2 dc) in same ch sp as beg sl st, work 20 sc in beg ch-15 sp, join with sl st in next sc. Fasten off. ■

Fig. 1
Straight Stitch

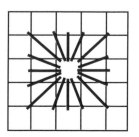

Daisy Pot Holder
Embroidery Diagram

Diagonal Shells
Pot Holder

DESIGN BY **ELIZABETH WHITE**

SKILL LEVEL

EASY

FINISHED SIZE
7 inches square, not including hanging lp

MATERIALS
- Pisgah Yarn and Dyeing Co., Inc. America's Best size 10 crochet cotton (150 yds per ball): 1 ball each #50 plum and #41 light peach
- Size 5/1.90mm steel crochet hook or size needed to obtain gauge

GAUGE
3 shell rows = 1 inch

PATTERN NOTE
Chain-3 at beginning of row counts as first double crochet unless otherwise stated.

SPECIAL STITCHES
Beginning shell (beg shell): Ch 3, 2 dc in same st.

Shell: (Sl st, ch 3, 2 dc) in next ch-3 sp.

INSTRUCTIONS
SIDE
MAKE 2.
Row 1: With plum, ch 4, 3 dc in 4th ch from hook, turn.

Row 2: Beg shell (see Special Stitches), sk next 2 sts, **shell** (see Special Stitches) in next ch-3 sp, turn.

Rows 3–15: Beg shell, shell across, turn. Fasten off at end of last row.

Row 16: Join light peach with sl st in first st, beg shell in same st as sl st, shell across, turn.

Row 17: Beg shell, shell across, turn. Fasten off.

Row 18: Join plum with sl st in first st, beg shell in same st as sl st, shell across, turn.

Row 19: Beg shell, shell across, turn. Fasten off.

Row 20: Join light peach with sl st in first st, beg shell in same st as sl st, shell across, turn.

Row 21: Beg shell, shell across, turn.

Row 22: Sl st in each of first 2 sts, (sl st, beg shell) in next ch-3 sp, shell across to last shell, sl st in ch-3 sp of last shell, turn. Fasten off.

Row 23: Join plum with sl st in ch sp of first shell, beg shell in same sp as last sl st, shell across to last shell, sl st in ch sp of last shell, turn.

Row 24: Sl st in each of first 2 sts, (sl st, beg shell) in first ch-3 sp, shell across to last shell, sl st in last shell, turn. Fasten off.

Row 25: Join light peach with sl st in first ch sp, beg shell in same sp as last sl st, shell across to last shell, sl st in ch sp of last shell, turn.

Row 26: Sl st in each of first 2 sts, (sl st, beg shell) in first ch-3 sp, shell across to last shell, sl st in last shell, turn. Fasten off.

Row 27: Join plum with sl st in first ch-3 sp, beg shell in same sp as last sl st, shell across to last shell, sl st in ch sp of last shell, turn.

Rows 28–39: Sl st in each of first 2 sts, (sl st, beg shell) in first ch-3 sp, shell across to last shell, sl st in last shell, turn.

Row 40: Sl st in each of first 2 sts, (sl st, beg shell) in first ch-3 sp, shell, sl st in last shell, turn.

Row 41: Sl st in each of first 2 sts, (sl st, beg shell) in first ch-3 sp, sl st in last shell. Fasten off.

EDGING
Holding Sides WS tog, matching sts, working through both thicknesses, join light peach with sc in end of last row, (for **hanging lp**, ch 15, shell) in same row as first sc, shell around, shell in same row as first sc, 20 sc in ch-15 sp, join with sl st in beg sc. Fasten off. ■

Basket Pot Holder

DESIGN BY ELIZABETH WHITE

SKILL LEVEL

EASY

FINISHED SIZE
7 x 7½ inches

MATERIALS
- Pisgah Yarn and Dyeing Co., Inc. America's Best size 10 crochet cotton (150 yds per ball): 1 ball each #89 camel, #120 fudge and #46 rose
- Size 5/1.90mm steel crochet hook or size needed to obtain gauge
- Tapestry needle

GAUGE
8 dc = 1 inch; 7 dc rows = 2 inches

PATTERN NOTE
Chain-3 at beginning of row counts as first double crochet unless otherwise stated.

INSTRUCTIONS
SIDE
MAKE 2.
Row 1: With camel, ch 27, dc in 4th ch from hook (*first 3 chs count as first dc*) and in each ch across, turn. (*25 dc*)

Row 2: Ch 3 (*see Pattern Note*), [sk next 2 sts, (dc, ch 2, dc) in next st] across to last 3 sts, sk next 2 sts, dc in last st, turn.

Rows 3 & 4: Ch 3, (2 dc, ch 2, 2 dc) in each sp across, dc in last st, turn.

Row 5: Ch 3, (3 dc, ch 2, 3 dc) in each ch sp across, dc in last st, turn.

Row 6: Ch 3, (3 dc, ch 2, 3 dc, ch 1) in each ch sp across to last ch sp, (3 dc, ch 2, 3 dc) in last ch sp, dc in last st, turn.

Row 7: Ch 3, *(3 dc, ch 2, 3 dc, ch 2) in next ch sp, sk next ch sp, rep from * across to last ch sp, (3 dc, ch 2, 3 dc) in last ch sp, dc in last st, turn.

Row 8: Ch 3, *(3 dc, ch 2, 3 dc, ch 3) in next ch sp, sk next ch sp, rep from * across to last ch sp, (3 dc, ch 2, 3 dc) in last ch sp, dc in last st, turn.

Row 9: Ch 3, *(3 dc, ch 2, 3 dc, ch 4) in next ch sp, sk next ch sp, rep from * across to last ch sp, (3 dc, ch 2, 3 dc) in last ch sp, dc in last st, turn.

Row 10: Ch 3, *(3 dc, ch 2, 3 dc, ch 5) in next ch sp, sk next ch sp, rep from * across to last ch sp, (3 dc, ch 2, 3 dc) in last ch sp, dc in last st, turn.

Row 11: Ch 3, (dc, ch 1) 7 times in next ch sp, [sc in next ch sp, ch 1, (dc, ch 1) 7 times in next ch sp] across to last st, dc in last st. Fasten off.

Row 12: Join fudge with sc in first ch sp, [ch 3, sc in next ch sp] across. Fasten off.

BASE
Row 1: Working in starting ch on opposite side of row 1, join camel with sl st in first ch, ch 3, sk next 2 chs, *(dc, ch 2, dc) in next ch, sk next 2 chs, rep from * across to last ch, dc in last ch, turn.

Rows 2 & 3: Ch 3, (2 dc, ch 2, 2 dc) in each ch sp across to last st, dc in last st, turn. Fasten off at end of last row.

EDGING

Hold Side pieces WS tog, matching sts, working through both thicknesses in sts and in ends of rows around outer edge, join fudge with sc in end of row 11, 2 sc in same row, 3 sc in end of each row, sc in each st and 2 sc in each ch sp around to opposite end of row 11. Fasten off.

HANDLE

Row 1: With camel, ch 22, dc in 4th ch from hook and in each ch across, turn. *(20 dc)*

Rows 2–6: Ch 2 *(does not count as a st)*, dc in each st across to last 2 sts, **dc dec** *(see Stitch Guide)* in last 2 sts, turn. *(10 dc at end of last row)*

Rows 7–18: Ch 3, dc in each st across, turn.

Rows 19–23: Ch 3, dc in same st, dc in each st across with 2 dc in last st, turn. *(20 dc at end of last row)*

Row 24: Ch 3, dc in each st across. Fasten off.

EDGING

Join fudge with sc in end of first row on 1 side of Handle, 2 sc in same row, 3 sc in end of each row across. Fasten off.

Rep on opposite side of Handle.

Sew ends of Handle centered to inside of row 10 on Sides.

ROSE

Rnd 1: With rose, ch 4, sl st in beg ch to form ring, ch 1, (sc, ch 3) 6 times in ring, join with sl st in beg sc. *(6 sc, 6 ch sps)*

Rnd 2: For **petals**, ch 1, (sc, ch 1, 3 dc, ch 1, sc) in each ch sp around, join with sl st in beg sc.

Rnd 3: Working behind petals, ch 3, [sc in **back strands** *(see Fig. 1)* of first sc on next petal, ch 3] around, join with sl st in first ch of beg ch-3.

Rnd 4: For **petals**, ch 1, (sc, ch 1, 5 dc, ch 1, sc) in each ch sp around, join with sl st in beg sc.

Rnd 5: Working behind petals, ch 5, [sc in back strands of first sc on next petal, ch 5] around, join with sl st in first ch of beg ch-5.

Rnd 6: For **petals**, ch 1, (sc, ch 1, 7 dc, ch 1, sc) in each ch sp around, join with sl st in beg sc. Fasten off.

Sew rose to front as shown in photo. ■

Fig. 1
Back Strands of
Single Crochet

Wild Rose
Dishcloth
DESIGN BY **SHERI L. JACOBSON**

SKILL LEVEL

EASY

FINISHED SIZE
10½ inches in diameter

MATERIALS
- Pisgah Yarn and Dyeing Co., Inc. Peaches & Crème medium (worsted) weight yarn (2½ oz/ 122 yds/70g per ball):
    1 ball each #56 celery, #123 lemon, #10 yellow and #45 pastel pink
- Size G/6/4mm crochet hook or size needed to obtain gauge

4 MEDIUM

GAUGE
4 dc = 1 inch; 2 dc rows = 1 inch

PATTERN NOTES
Join with slip stitch as indicated unless otherwise stated.

Chain-3 at beginning of round counts as first double crochet unless otherwise stated.

INSTRUCTIONS
DISHCLOTH
Rnd 1: With lemon, ch 3, **join** (see Pattern Notes) in beg ch to form ring, **ch 3** (see Pattern Notes), 14 dc in ring, join in 3rd ch of beg ch-3. (15 dc)

Rnd 2: Working this rnd in **front lps** (see Stitch Guide), join yellow in any st, ch 4, [sl st in next st, ch 4] around, join in joining sl st of last rnd. Fasten off.

Rnd 3: Working in **back lps** (see Stitch Guide) of rnd 1, join pastel pink in any st, ch 3, dc in same st, 2 dc in each st around, join in 3rd ch of beg ch 3. (30 dc)

Rnd 4: Ch 3, dc in same st, [dc in next st, 2 dc in next st] twice, ch 1, sk next st, *2 dc in next st, [dc in next st, 2 dc in next st] twice, ch 1, sk next st, rep from * around, join in 3rd ch of beg ch-3. (40 dc, 5 ch-1 sps)

Rnd 5: Ch 1, sc in first st, *hdc in next st, 2 dc in each of next 4 sts, hdc in next st, sc in next st, sl st in next ch sp**, sc in next st, rep from * around, ending last rep at **, join in beg sc. Fasten off.

Rnd 6: Working behind rnds 4 and 5, join celery in any sk st on rnd 3, ch 11 (counts as first dc and ch-8 sp), [dc in next sk st, ch 8] around, join in 3rd ch of beg ch-11.

Rnd 7: Ch 1, working over sl sts of last rnd, sc in corresponding ch sp on rnd 5 between petals, [sc in each of next 7 chs, 2 sc in next ch, sc in next ch sp between petals, sk next dc, sc in each of next 8 chs, sc in next ch sp between petals, sk next dc] twice, sc in each of next 7 chs, 2 sc in last ch, join in beg sc. (48 sts)

Rnd 8: Ch 3, dc in same st, dc in each of next 2 sts, [ch 1, dc in each of next 7 sts] 6 times, ch 1, dc in each of last 3 sts, join in 3rd ch of beg ch-3. (49 dc, 7 ch sps)

Rnd 9: Ch 3, dc in next st, *dc dec (*see Stitch Guide*) in next 2 sts, ch 3, dc in next ch-1 sp, ch 3, dc dec in next 2 sts**, dc in each of next 3 sts, rep from * around, ending last rep at **, dc in last st, join in 3rd ch of beg ch-3. (*42 dc, 14 ch sps*)

Rnd 10: Ch 3, *dc dec in next 2 sts, ch 3, sk next ch sp, 5 dc in next dc, ch 3, sk next ch sp, dc dec in next 2 sts**, dc in next st, rep from * around, ending last rep at **, join in 3rd ch of beg ch-3. (*56 dc, 14 ch sps*)

Rnd 11: Sl st in next st, sl st in each of next 3 chs, sl st in next dc, ch 3, 2 dc in same st, *dc in each of next 3 sts, 3 dc in next st, ch 3, sk next ch sp, dc dec in next 3 sts, ch 3, sk next ch sp**, 3 dc in next st, rep from * around, ending last rep at **, join in 3rd ch of beg ch-3.

Rnd 12: Ch 3, 2 dc in same st, *dc in each of next 7 sts, 3 dc in next st, ch 2, sk next ch sp, sc in next st, ch 2, sk next ch sp**, 3 dc in next st, rep from * around, ending last rep at **, join in 3rd ch of beg ch-3.

Rnd 13: Ch 3, 5 dc in same st, *sk next 2 sts, sc in next st, ch 2, sk next 2 sts, (dc, ch 2, dc) in next st, ch 2, sk next 2 sts, sc in next st, sk next 2 sts, 6 dc in next st, sk next 2 ch sps**, 6 dc in next st, rep from * around, ending last rep at **, join in 3rd ch of beg ch-3. Fasten off. ■

Wild Rose Scrubbie

DESIGN BY **SHERI L. JACOBSON**

SKILL LEVEL

EASY

FINISHED SIZE
5 inches in diameter, not including hanger

MATERIALS
- Pisgah Yarn and Dyeing Co., Inc. Peaches & Crème medium (worsted) weight yarn (2½ oz/ 122 yds/70g per ball):
    1 ball each #56 celery, #123 lemon, #10 yellow and #45 pastel pink
- Size G/6/4mm crochet hook or size needed to obtain gauge
- Tapestry needle
- 1-inch plastic ring
- Safety pins
- Plastic mesh pot scrubber

4 MEDIUM

GAUGE
4 dc = 1 inch; 2 dc rows = 1 inch

PATTERN NOTES
Join with slip stitch as indicated unless otherwise stated.

Chain-3 at beginning of round counts as first double crochet unless otherwise stated.

INSTRUCTIONS
SCRUBBIE

Rnd 1: With lemon, ch 3, **join** *(see Pattern Notes)* in beg ch to form ring, **ch 3** *(see Pattern Notes)*, 14 dc in ring, join in 3rd ch of beg ch-3. *(15 dc)*

Rnd 2: Working this rnd in **front lps** *(see Stitch Guide)*, join yellow in any st, ch 4, [sl st in next st, ch 4) around, join in joining sl st of last rnd. Fasten off.

Rnd 3: Working in **back lps** *(see Stitch Guide)* of rnd 1, join pastel pink in any st, ch 3, dc in same st, 2 dc in each st around, join in 3rd ch of beg ch 3. *(30 dc)*

Rnd 4: Ch 3, dc in same st, [dc in next st, 2 dc in next st] twice, ch 1, sk next st, *2 dc in next st, [dc in next st, 2 dc in next st] twice, ch 1, sk next st, rep from * around, join in 3rd ch of beg ch-3. *(40 dc, 5 ch-1 sps)*

Rnd 5: Ch 1, sc in first st, *hdc in next st, 2 dc in each of next 4 sts, hdc in next st, sc in next st, sl st in next ch sp**, sc in next st, rep from * around, ending last rep at **, join in beg sc. Fasten off.

Rnd 6: Working behind rnds 4 and 5, join celery in any sk st on rnd 3, ch 11 *(counts as first dc and ch-8 sp)*, [dc in next sk st, ch 8] around, join in 3rd ch of beg ch-11.

Note: Using safety pins, pin round 6 to outer edge of plastic scrubber. Remove pins as you join flower to scrubber.

Rnd 7: Ch 1, *[insert hook in next ch on ch-8 and under 5 or 6 plastic mesh strands, yo, pull lp through, complete as sc] 8 times, rep from * around, join in beg sc. Fasten off.

LEAF
MAKE 2.

With celery, ch 9, hdc in 3rd ch from hook, dc in next ch, 2 tr in each of next 2 chs, dc in next ch, hdc in next ch, (sc, ch 2, sc) in last ch, working on opposite side of ch, hdc in next ch, dc in next ch, 2 tr in each of next 2 chs, dc in next ch, hdc in last ch. Fasten off, leaving long strand for sewing.

Sew Leaves side by side to last rnd of Scrubbie.

HANGER

Join celery with **sc in plastic ring** *(see Fig. 1)*, 19 sc in ring, join in beg sc. Fasten off, leaving long strand for sewing.

Sew to last rnd of Scrubbie opposite Leaves. ∎

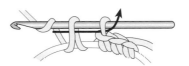

Fig. 1
Single Crochet Over Ring

Poinsettia Scrubbie

DESIGN BY **SHERI L. JACOBSON**

SKILL LEVEL

EASY

FINISHED SIZE

5½ inches across

MATERIALS

- Pisgah Yarn and Dyeing Co., Inc. Peaches & Crème medium (worsted) weight yarn (2½ oz/ 122 yds/70g per ball):
  1 ball each #95 red, #12 gold and #65 Christmas green
- Size G/6/4mm crochet hook or size needed to obtain gauge
- Tapestry needle
- 1-inch plastic ring
- Safety pins
- Plastic mesh pot scrubber

GAUGE

Rnds 1–4 = 3½ inches across

PATTERN NOTES

Join with slip stitch as indicated unless otherwise stated.

Chain-3 at beginning of round counts as first double crochet unless otherwise stated.

INSTRUCTIONS
SCRUBBIE

Rnd 1: With gold, ch 3, **join** (see Pattern Notes) in beg ch to form ring, ch 1, 7 sc in ring, join in beg sc. (7 sc)

Rnd 2: Working this rnd in **front lps** (see Stitch Guide), ch 1, sc in first st, ch 3, (sc in next st, ch 3) around, join in beg sc. Fasten off. (7 sc, 7 ch sps)

Rnd 3: Working this rnd in **back lps** (see Stitch Guide) of rnd 1, join red with sc in any st, sc in same st, 2 sc in each st around, join in beg sc. (14 sc)

Rnd 4: Ch 1, sc in front lp of first st, *for **petal**, ch 5, sc in 2nd ch from hook, hdc in next ch, dc in next ch, hdc in next ch, sk next sc**, sc in front lp of next sc, rep from * around, ending last rep at **, join in beg sc. Fasten off. (7 petals)

Rnd 5: Working in back lps of rnd 3, join red in any st, **ch 3** (see Pattern Notes), dc in same st, 2 dc in each st around to last st, dc in last st, join in 3rd ch of beg ch-3. (27 dc)

Rnd 6: Ch 1, sc in front lp of each of first 2 sts, *ch 5, sc in 2nd ch from hook, hdc in next ch, dc in next ch, tr in next ch, dc in side of last sc made before ch-5, sk next dc on rnd 5**, sc in front lp of each of next 2 sts, rep from * around, ending last rep at **, join in beg sc. Fasten off.

Rnd 7: Working in back lps of rnd 5, join Christmas green in any st, ch 3, [2 dc in next st, dc in next st] around, join in 3rd ch of beg ch-3. (40 dc)

Note: Using safety pins, pin rnd 7 to outer edge of plastic scrubber. Remove pins when needed as you work.

Rnd 8: Ch 1, insert hook in first st and under 5 or 6 plastic mesh strands, yo, complete as sc, [insert hook in next st and under 5 or 6 plastic mesh strands, yo, complete as sc] around, join in beg sc. Fasten off.

LEAF
MAKE 2.

With Christmas green, ch 11, tr in 4th ch from hook, 2 tr in next ch, dc in next ch, hdc in next ch, 2 dc in next ch, dc in next ch, hdc in next ch, (sc, ch 3, sl st in 2nd ch from hook, ch 1, sc) in last ch, working on opposite side of ch, hdc in next ch, dc in next ch, 2 dc in next ch, hdc in next ch, dc in next ch, 2 tr in next ch, tr in next ch, dc in last ch. Fasten off, leaving long strand for sewing.

Sew Leaves side by side to last rnd of Scrubbie.

HANGER

Join Christmas green with **sc in plastic ring** *(see Fig. 1)*, 19 sc in ring, join in beg sc. Fasten off, leaving long strand for sewing.

Sew to last rnd of Scrubbie opposite Leaves. ■

Fig. 1
Single Crochet Over Ring

Dress
Pot Holder
DESIGN BY **ELIZABETH WHITE**

SKILL LEVEL

EASY

FINISHED SIZE
8 x 10½ inches, not including hanger

MATERIALS
- Pisgah Yarn and Dyeing Co., Inc. America's Best size 10 crochet cotton (white: 225 yds per ball; ombre: 150 yds per ball):
  1 ball each #1 white and #151 fairy tales
- Size 5/1.90mm steel crochet hook or size needed to obtain gauge
- Tapestry needle

GAUGE
7 dc = 1 inch; 7 dc rows = 2 inches

PATTERN NOTES
Join with slip stitch as indicated unless otherwise stated.

Chain-3 at beginning of round counts as first double crochet unless otherwise stated.

INSTRUCTIONS
DRESS
Rnd 1: With fairy tales, ch 40, **join** (see Pattern Notes) in beg ch to form ring, **ch 3** (see Pattern Notes), dc in same ch, dc in next ch, [2 dc in next ch, dc in next ch] around, join in 3rd ch of beg ch-3. (60 dc)

Rnd 2: Ch 3, dc in same st, dc in each of next 2 sts, [2 dc in next st, dc in each of next 2 sts] around, join in 3rd ch of beg ch-3. (80 dc)

Rnd 3: Ch 3, dc in same st, dc in each of next 3 sts, [2 dc in next st, dc in each of next 3 sts] around, join in 3rd ch of beg ch-3. (100 dc)

Rnd 4: Ch 3, dc in same st, dc in each of next 4 sts, [2 dc in next st, dc in each of next 4 sts] around, join in 3rd ch of beg ch-3. (120 dc)

Rnd 5: Ch 3, dc in same st, dc in each of next 5 sts, [2 dc in next st, dc in each of next 5 sts] around, join in 3rd ch of beg ch-3. (140 dc)

Rnd 6: Ch 5 (counts as first dc and ch-2 sp), dc in same st, [sk next 2 sts, (dc, ch 2, dc) in next st] 11 times, for **armhole**, sk next 36 sts, (dc, ch 2, dc) in next st, rep between [ ] 11 times, for **armhole**, sk last 36 sts, join in 3rd ch of beg ch-5.

Rnd 7: (Sl st, ch 3, dc, ch 2, 2 dc) in first ch sp, (2 dc, ch 2, 2 dc) in each ch sp around, join in 3rd ch of beg ch-3.

Rnd 8: Sl st in next st, (sl st, ch 3, dc, ch 2, 2 dc) in first ch sp, ch 1, (2 dc, ch 2, 2 dc, ch 1) in each ch sp around, join in 3rd ch of beg ch-3.

Rnd 9: Sl st in next st, (sl st, ch 3, 2 dc, ch 2, 3 dc) in first ch sp, ch 1, sk next ch sp, *(3 dc, ch 2, 3 dc) in next ch sp, ch 1, sk next ch sp, rep from * around, join in 3rd ch of beg ch-3.

Rnds 10–18: Sl st in each of next 2 sts, (sl st, ch 3, 2 dc, ch 2, 3 dc, ch 1) in first ch sp, sk next ch sp, *(3 dc, ch 2, 3 dc, ch 1) in next ch sp, sk next ch sp, rep from * around, join in 3rd ch of beg ch-3. Fasten off at end of last rnd.

Rnd 19: Join white with sc in last ch sp, ch 1, (dc, ch 1) 5 times in next ch sp, [sc in next ch sp, ch 1, (dc, ch 1) 5 times in next ch sp] around, join in beg sc.

Row 20: Sl st in next ch sp, ch 1, sc in same sp, ch 3, [sc in next ch sp, ch 3] around, join in beg sc. Fasten off.

BODICE RUFFLE
Rnd 1: Working around posts of sts on rnd 5, join white with sc around first st, ch 3, sk next st, [sc around next st, ch 3, sk next st] around, join in beg sc.

Rnd 2: Ch 1, sc in first ch sp, ch 3, [sc next ch sp, ch 3] around, join in beg sc. Fasten off.

Flatten Dress, working in starting ch on opposite side of row 1 through all thicknesses, join white with sc in first ch, sc in each ch across, for **hanger**, ch 15, sl st in same st as last sc. Fasten off. ∎

Diamonds **Pot Holder**

DESIGN BY **JUDY TEAGUE TREECE**

SKILL LEVEL

EASY

FINISHED SIZE

10 x 11 inches, not including hanging lp

MATERIALS

- Size 3 crochet cotton:
  190 yds blue
  100 yds white
  10 yds pink
- Size F/5/3.75mm crochet hook
  or size needed to obtain gauge

GAUGE

9 sc = 2 inches; 11 sc rows = 2 inches;
2 sc rows and 1 fpdc row = 1 inch

INSTRUCTIONS
FRONT

Row 1 (RS): With white, ch 44, sc in 2nd ch from hook and in each ch across, turn. *(43 sc)*

Row 2: Ch 1, sc in each st across, turn.

Row 3: Ch 1, sc in each st across, **do not turn**. Fasten off.

Rnd 4 (RS): With RS facing, join blue with sc in first st, [sc in next st, **fpdc** *(see Stitch Guide)* around next st on row before last, sk next st on this row, **fptr** *(see Stitch Guide)* around next st 3 rows below, sk next st on last row, fpdc around next st on row before last, sk next st on last row] across to last 2 sts, sc in each of last 2 sts, turn.

Row 5: Ch 1, sc in each st across, turn.

Row 6: Ch 1, sc in each st across, **do not turn**. Fasten off.

Row 7 (RS): With RS facing, join white with sc in first st, fptr around next st 3 rows below, sk next st on last row, [fpdc around next st on row before last, sk next st on last row, sc in next st, fpdc around next st on row before last, sk next st on last row, fptr around next st 3 rows below, sk next st on last row] across to last st, sc in last st, turn.

Rows 8–49: [Rep rows 2–7 consecutively] 7 times. **Do not turn** at end of last row.

Rnd 50: Now working in rnds around outer edge in sts and ends of rows, ch 1, sk first row, sc in each row across to last row, sk last row, working in starting ch on opposite side of row 1, 3 sc in first ch, sc in each ch across with 3 sc in last ch, sk first row, sc in each row across to last row, sk last row, 3 sc in first st, sc in each st across with 3 sc in last st, join with sl st in beg sc. Fasten off. *(188 sc)*

BACK

Row 1: With blue, ch 44, sc in 2nd ch from hook and in each ch across, turn. *(43 sc)*

Rows 2–49: Ch 1, sc in each st across, turn. **Do not turn** at end of last row.

Rnd 50: Rep rnd 50 of Front.

BORDER

Rnd 1: Holding Front and Back WS tog with Front facing, matching sts, working through both thicknesses, join pink with sc in any center corner st, 2 sc in same st, sc in each st around with 3 sc in each center corner st, join with sl st in beg sc. Fasten off.

Rnd 2: Join white with sc in top left-hand corner st, sc in same st, **turn**, for **hanging lp**, (sl st, ch 10, sl st) in next st, **turn**, ch 1, 20 sc in ch lp just made, sl st in next st, sc in each st around with 3 sc in each center corner st, sc in same st as first sc, join with sl st in beg sc. Fasten off. ■

Double Corner Pot Holder

DESIGN BY **ELIZABETH WHITE**

SKILL LEVEL
EASY

FINISHED SIZE
6½ inches square, not including hanging lp

MATERIALS
- Pisgah Yarn and Dyeing Co., Inc. America's Best size 10 crochet cotton (150 yds per ball): 1 ball each #10 yellow and #467 khaki
- Size 5/1.90mm steel crochet hook or size needed to obtain gauge

GAUGE
7 dc = 1 inch; 7 dc rows = 2 inches

PATTERN NOTE
Chain-3 at beginning of row counts as first double crochet unless otherwise stated.

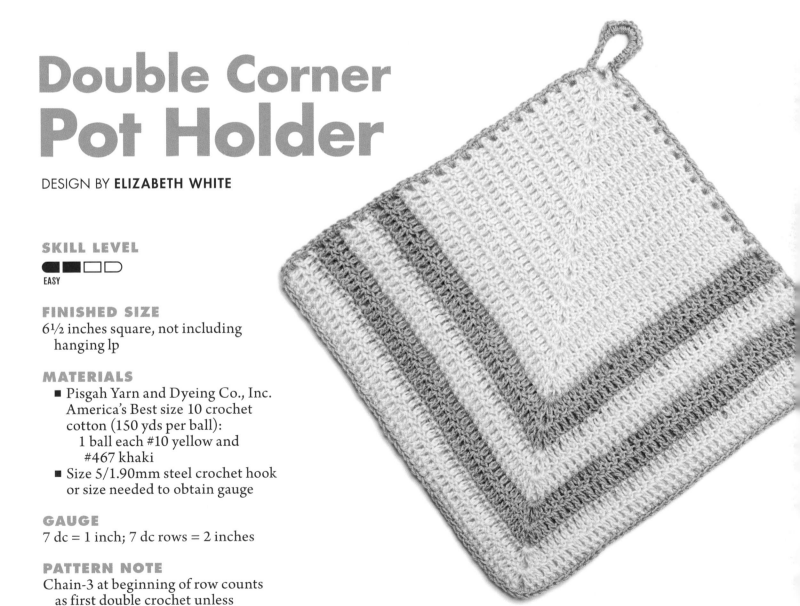

INSTRUCTIONS
SIDE
MAKE 2.
Row 1: With yellow, ch 6, sl st in beg ch to form ring, **ch 3** *(see Pattern Note)*, (3 dc, ch 2, 4 dc) in ring, turn. *(8 dc, 1 ch sp)*

Rows 2–14: Ch 3, dc in each st across with (2 dc, ch 2, 2 dc) in ch sp, turn. Fasten off at end of last row.

Row 15: Join khaki with sl st in first st, ch 3, dc in each st across with (2 dc, ch 2, 2 dc) in ch sp, turn.

Row 16: Ch 3, dc in each st across with (2 dc, ch 2, 2 dc) in ch sp, turn. Fasten off.

Row 17: Join yellow with sl st in first st, ch 3, dc in each st across with (2 dc, ch 2, 2 dc) in ch sp, turn.

Row 18: Ch 3, dc in each st across with (2 dc, ch 2, 2 dc) in ch sp, turn. Fasten off.

Row 19: Join khaki with sl st in first st, ch 3, dc in each st across with (2 dc, ch 2, 2 dc) in ch sp, turn.

Row 20: Ch 3, dc in each st across with (2 dc, ch 2, 2 dc) in ch sp, turn. Fasten off.

Row 21: Join yellow with sl st in first st, ch 3, dc in each st across with (2 dc, ch 2, 2 dc) in ch sp, turn.

Row 22: Ch 3, dc in each st across with (2 dc, ch 2, 2 dc) in ch sp, turn. Fasten off.

EDGING
Holding Sides WS tog, matching sts, working through both thicknesses, join khaki with sc in beg ring on opposite side of row 1, for **hanging lp**, ch 15, sc in same ring, 2 sc in end of each row, 2 sc in ch sp and sc in each st around to ch-15, 20 sc in ch-15, join with sl st in beg sc. Fasten off. ∎

Yellow Hot Pad

DESIGN BY **JO ANN LOFTIS**

SKILL LEVEL

EASY

FINISHED SIZE
9¼ inches across

MATERIALS
- Pisgah Yarn and Dyeing Co., Inc. Peaches & Crème medium (worsted) weight yarn (2½ oz/ 122 yds/70g per ball): 1 ball each #1 white and #3 cream
- Size I/9/5.5mm crochet hook or size needed to obtain gauge

GAUGE
With 2 strands held together: 3 sts = 1 inch

PATTERN NOTES
Join with slip stitch as indicated unless otherwise stated.

Chain-3 at beginning of round counts as first double crochet unless otherwise stated.

Work with 2 strands held together as 1 throughout.

SPECIAL STITCH
Cluster (cl): Yo, insert hook in designated st, yo, pull lp through, yo, pull through 2 lps on hook, yo, insert hook in same st, yo, pull lp through, yo, pull through 2 lps on hook, yo, pull through all 3 lps on hook.

INSTRUCTIONS
HOT PAD
Rnd 1: With white, ch 4, **join** *(see Pattern Notes)* in beg ch to form ring, ch 5 *(counts as first dc and ch-2 sp)*, dc in ring, ch 3, [dc in ring, ch 2, dc in ring, ch-3] 3 times, join in 3rd ch of beg ch-5. *(8 dc, 4 ch-2 sps, 4 ch-3 sps)*

Rnd 2: Ch 1, 3 sc in first ch-2 sp, 5 sc in next ch-3 sp, [3 sc in next ch-2 sp, 5 sc in next ch-3 sp] around, join in beg sc. Fasten off. *(32 sc)*

Rnd 3: Join cream in center st of any 3-sc group, ch 2, dc in same st *(counts as first cl)*, sk next 3 sts, *(**cl**—see Special Stitch, ch 4, cl) in next st, sk next 3 sts, (cl, ch 3, cl) in next st, sk next 3 sts, rep from * twice, (cl, ch 4, cl) in next st, sk next 3 sts, cl in same st as first st, ch 3, join in top of first dc.

Rnd 4: Ch 1, sc each of first 2 sts, [5 sc in next corner ch sp, sc in each of next 2 sts, 3 sc in next ch sp, sc in each of next 2 sts] 3 times, 5 sc in next corner ch sp, sc in each of next 2 sts, 3 sc in next ch sp, join in beg sc.

Rnd 5: Working this rnd in **back lps** *(see Stitch Guide)*, ch 4 *(counts as first tr)*, tr in each of next 3 sts, *(2 tr, ch 3, 2 tr) in next st, tr in each of next 11 sts, rep from * twice, (2 tr, ch 3, 2 tr) in next st, tr in each of last 7 sts, join in 4th ch of beg ch-4.

Rnd 6: (Sl st, ch 1, sc) in next st, sk next 3 sts, *(tr, {ch 1, tr} 7 times) in next ch sp, sk next 3 sts, sc in next st, sk next 3 sts, (tr, {ch 1, tr} 4 times) in next st, sk next 3 sts, sc in next st, sk next 3 sts, rep from * twice, (tr {ch 1, tr} 7 times) in next ch sp, sk next 3 sts, sc in next st, sk next 3 sts, (tr {ch 1, tr} 4 times) in next st, sk next st, join in beg sc. Fasten off.

Rnd 7: Join white with sc in any sc, 2 sc in each ch-1 sp and sc in each sc around, join in beg sc. Fasten off. ■

Starburst Dishcloth

DESIGN BY **DEBORAH LEVI-HAMBURG**

SKILL LEVEL

EASY

FINISHED SIZE
8 x 12½ inches

MATERIALS
- Medium (worsted) weight cotton yarn:
  2 oz/100 yds/56g each yellow and orange
  1½ oz/75 yds/42g green
- Size G/6/4mm crochet hook or size needed to obtain gauge

GAUGE
2 7-dc groups and 3 sc = 3½ inches; 2 dc rows and 1 sc row = 2 inches

PATTERN NOTE
Chain-3 at beginning of row counts as first double crochet unless otherwise stated.

INSTRUCTIONS
DISHCLOTH
Row 1: With orange, ch 37, sc in 2nd ch from hook and in each ch across, turn. *(36 sc)*

Row 2: Ch 1, sc in each of first 2 sts, [sk next 3 sts, 7 dc in next st, sk next 3 sts, sc in each of next 3 sts] 3 times, sk next 3 sts, 4 dc in last st, turn. Fasten off. *(36 sts)*

Row 3: Join yellow with sc in first st, sc in next st, **dc dec** *(see Stitch Guide)* in next 7 sts, [sc in each of next 3 sts, dc dec in next 7 sts] twice, sc in each of next 3 sts, dc dec in last 4 sts, turn. *(15 sts)*

Row 4: Ch 3 *(see Pattern Note)*, 3 dc in same st, [sc in each of next 3 sts, 7 dc in next st] 3 times, sc in each of last 2 sts, turn. Fasten off. *(36 sts)*

Row 5: Join green with sl st in first st, ch 3 *(does not count as a st)*, dc dec in next 3 sts, [sc in each of next 3 sts, dc dec in next 7 sts] 3 times, sc in each of last 2 sts, turn. *(15 sts)*

Row 6: Ch 1, sc in each of first 2 sts, [7 dc in next st, sc in each of next 3 sts] 3 times, 4 dc in last st, turn. Fasten off.

Row 7: Join yellow with sc in first st, sc in next st, dc dec in next 7 sts, [sc in each of next 3 sts, dc dec in next 7 sts] twice, sc in each of next 3 sts, dc dec in last 4 sts, turn. *(15 sts)*

Row 8: Ch 3, 3 dc in same st, [sc in each of next 3 sts, 7 dc in next st] 3 times, sc in each of last 2 sts, turn. Fasten off. *(36 sts)*

Row 9: Join orange with sl st in first st, ch 3, *(does not count as a st)*, dc dec in next 3 sts, [sc in each of next 3 sts, dc dec in next 7 sts] 3 times, sc in each of last 2 sts, turn. *(15 sts)*

Row 10: Ch 1, sc in each of first 2 sts, [7 dc in next st, sc in each of next 3 sts] 3 times, 4 dc in last st, turn. Fasten off.

Rows 11–18: Rep rows 3–10.

Rows 19–25: Rep rows 3–9.

Row 26: Ch 1, sc in each of first 2 sts, [2 sc in sp before next dc, sc in next dc, 2 sc in sp after same dc, sc in each of next 3 sts] 3 times, 2 sc in sp before next dc, sc in next dc, sc in 3rd ch of last ch-3, turn.

Row 27: Ch 1, sc in each st across. Fasten off. ∎

Nylon
SCRUBBIES

DESIGN BY **DARLA FANTON**

SKILL LEVEL

EASY

FINISHED SIZE
3½ inches in diameter

MATERIALS
- 72-inch-wide coarse nylon netting: ½ yd of each green and ecru
- Size K/10½/6.5mm double-ended crochet hook or size needed to obtain gauge
- Tapestry needle
- Cutting mat and rotary cutter
- Monofilament line

GAUGE
4 sts = 1 inch; 4 rows = 4 inches

PATTERN NOTES
To **pull up a lp**, insert hook in designated lp, bar or st, yo, pull lp through, leaving lp on hook.

To **add a new color**, place sl st on hook with new color, pull sl st through 1 lp on hook, [yo, pull through 2 lps on hook] across, **or**, when using a color already in use, pick up color from row before and work lps off hook. Last lp on hook is first vertical bar of next row.

To **work lps off hook**, yo, pull through 1 lp on hook, [yo, pull through 2 lps on hook] across.

INSTRUCTIONS
SCRUBBIE

Notes: Cut netting into 2-inch wide strips. When attaching strips, overlap 1 inch at ends and continue working.

Row 1: With green, ch 30, **pull up a lp** *(see Pattern Notes)* in 2nd ch from hook and in each ch across, turn. *(30 lps on hook)*

Row 2: With ecru, **work lps off hook** *(see Pattern Notes)*, **do not turn**.

Row 3: Ch 1, pull up lp in top strand of each **horizontal bar** *(see Fig. 1)* across, turn.

Fig. 1
Horizontal Bar

Row 4: With green, work lps off hook, **do not turn**.

Row 5: Ch 1, pull up lp in top strand of each horizontal bar across, turn.

Row 6: With ecru, work lps off hook, **do not turn**.

Row 7: Ch 1, pull up lp in top strand of each horizontal bar across, turn.

Rows 8–23: [Rep rows 4–7 consecutively] 4 times.

Row 24: Rep row 4.

Row 25: Sl st in top strand of each horizontal bar across. Fasten off.

With green, sew short edges tog, forming a tube.

Using monofilament line, sew openings closed at each end, stuffing with nylon netting before closing. Secure end. ■

Dishcloth

DESIGN BY **JANE PEARSON**

SKILL LEVEL

BEGINNER

FINISHED SIZE
9½ x 11 inches

MATERIALS
- Pisgah Yarn and Dyeing Co., Inc. Peaches & Crème medium (worsted) weight yarn (solid: 2½ oz/122 yds/70g per ball; ombre: 2 oz/98 yds/56g per ball): 1 ball each #131 orange sherbet and #42 tea rose
- Size G/6/4mm crochet hook or size needed to obtain gauge

GAUGE
7 sc = 2 inches; 10 rows = 2½ inches

INSTRUCTIONS
DISHCLOTH
Row 1: With orange sherbet, ch 31, sc in 2nd ch from hook and in each ch across, turn. *(30 sc)*

Rows 2–40: Ch 1, sc in each st across, turn. Fasten off at end of last row.

EDGING
Rnd 1: Join tea rose with sc in first st, 2 sc in same st, sc in each st and in end of each row around with 3 sc in each corner st, join with sl st in beg sc. *(148 sc)*

Rnd 2: Ch 1, (sc, dc) in first st, sk next st, *(sc, dc) in next st, sk next st, rep from * around, join with sl st in beg sc. Fasten off. ∎

Starfish Hot Pad

DESIGN BY **JO ANN LOFTIS**

SKILL LEVEL

EASY

FINISHED SIZE

10 inches across, point to point

MATERIALS

- Pisgah Yarn and Dyeing Co., Inc.
  Peaches & Crème medium
  (worsted) weight yarn (2½ oz/
  122 yds/70g per ball):
    2 balls #55 light green
    1 ball #1 white
- Size I/9/5.5mm crochet hook
  or size needed to obtain gauge

GAUGE

With 2 strands held tog: 3 sts = 1 inch

PATTERN NOTES

Join with slip stitch as indicated unless
  otherwise stated.

Chain-3 at beginning of round counts as first
  double crochet unless otherwise stated.

Work with 2 strands held together as
  1 throughout.

INSTRUCTIONS

HOT PAD

Rnd 1: With light green, ch 4, **join** (see Pattern
Notes) in beg ch to form ring, ch 1, 12 sc in ring,
join in beg sc. (12 sc)

Rnds 2 & 3: **Ch 3** (see Pattern Notes), dc in same
st, 2 dc in each st around, join in 3rd ch of beg
ch-3. (24 dc, 48 dc)

Rnd 4: Ch 3, 2 dc in same st, sc in each of next
7 sts, [3 dc in next st, sc in each of next 7 sts]
around, join in 3rd ch of beg ch-3. (18 dc, 42 sc)

Rnd 5: (Sl st, ch 3, 2 dc) in next st, sc in each
of next 9 sts, [3 dc in next st, sc in each of
next 9 sts] around, join in 3rd ch of beg ch-3.
(18 dc, 54 sc)

Rnd 6: (Sl st, ch 3, 2 dc) in next st, sc in each of
next 11 sts, [3 dc in next st, sc in each of next
11 sts] around, join in 3rd ch of beg ch-3.
Fasten off. (18 dc, 66 sc)

Rnd 7: Join white with sc in first st, 2 sc in next
st, sc in each st around with 2 sc in center st of
each 3-dc group, join in beg sc. Fasten off. ■

Metric
Conversion
Charts

METRIC CONVERSIONS

yards	x	.9144	=	metres (m)
yards	x	91.44	=	centimetres (cm)
inches	x	2.54	=	centimetres (cm)
inches	x	25.40	=	millimetres (mm)
inches	x	.0254	=	metres (m)

centimetres	x	.3937	=	inches
metres	x	1.0936	=	yards

INCHES INTO MILLIMETRES & CENTIMETRES (Rounded off slightly)

inches	mm	cm	inches	cm	inches	cm	inches	cm
1/8	3	0.3	5	12.5	21	53.5	38	96.5
1/4	6	0.6	5 1/2	14	22	56	39	99
3/8	10	1	6	15	23	58.5	40	101.5
1/2	13	1.3	7	18	24	61	41	104
5/8	15	1.5	8	20.5	25	63.5	42	106.5
3/4	20	2	9	23	26	66	43	109
7/8	22	2.2	10	25.5	27	68.5	44	112
1	25	2.5	11	28	28	71	45	114.5
1 1/4	32	3.2	12	30.5	29	73.5	46	117
1 1/2	38	3.8	13	33	30	76	47	119.5
1 3/4	45	4.5	14	35.5	31	79	48	122
2	50	5	15	38	32	81.5	49	124.5
2 1/2	65	6.5	16	40.5	33	84	50	127
3	75	7.5	17	43	34	86.5		
3 1/2	90	9	18	46	35	89		
4	100	10	19	48.5	36	91.5		
4 1/2	115	11.5	20	51	37	94		

KNITTING NEEDLES CONVERSION CHART

Canada/U.S.	0	1	2	3	4	5	6	7	8	9	10	10½	11	13	15
Metric (mm)	2	2¼	2¾	3¼	3½	3¾	4	4½	5	5½	6	6½	8	9	10

CROCHET HOOKS CONVERSION CHART

Canada/U.S.	1/B	2/C	3/D	4/E	5/F	6/G	8/H	9/I	10/J	10½/K	N
Metric (mm)	2.25	2.75	3.25	3.5	3.75	4.25	5	5.5	6	6.5	9.0

Annie's Attic®

Big Book of Dishcloths, Pot Holders & Scrubbies is published by DRG, 306 East Parr Road, Berne, IN 46711.
Printed in USA. Copyright © 2009 DRG. All rights reserved. This publication may not be reproduced
in part or in whole without written permission from the publisher.

RETAIL STORES: If you would like to carry this pattern book or any other DRG publications, visit DRGwholesale.com

Every effort has been made to ensure that the instructions in this publication are complete and accurate.
We cannot, however, take responsibility for human error, typographical mistakes or variations in individual work.
Please visit AnniesCustomerCare.com to check for pattern updates.

ISBN: 978-1-59635-249-0

456789

Stitch Guide

For more complete information, visit **FreePatterns.com**

ABBREVIATIONS

beg	begin/begins/beginning
bpdc	back post double crochet
bpsc	back post single crochet
bptr	back post treble crochet
CC	contrasting color
ch(s)	chain(s)
ch-	refers to chain or space previously made (e.g., ch-1 space)
ch sp(s)	chain space(s)
cl(s)	cluster(s)
cm	centimeter(s)
dc	double crochet (singular/plural)
dc dec	double crochet 2 or more stitches together, as indicated
dec	decrease/decreases/decreasing
dtr	double treble crochet
ext	extended
fpdc	front post double crochet
fpsc	front post single crochet
fptr	front post treble crochet
g	gram(s)
hdc	half double crochet
hdc dec	half double crochet 2 or more stitches together, as indicated
inc	increase/increases/increasing
lp(s)	loop(s)
MC	main color
mm	millimeter(s)
oz	ounce(s)
pc	popcorn(s)
rem	remain/remains/remaining
rep(s)	repeat(s)
rnd(s)	round(s)
RS	right side
sc	single crochet (singular/plural)
sc dec	single crochet 2 or more stitches together, as indicated
sk	skip/skipped/skipping
sl st(s)	slip stitch(es)
sp(s)	space/spaces/spaced
st(s)	stitch(es)
tog	together
tr	treble crochet
trtr	triple treble
WS	wrong side
yd(s)	yard(s)
yo	yarn over

Chain—ch: Yo, pull through lp on hook.

Slip stitch—sl st: Insert hook in st, pull through both lps on hook.

Single crochet—sc: Insert hook in st, yo, pull through st, yo, pull through both lps on hook.

Front post stitch—fp: Back post stitch—bp: When working post st, insert hook from right to left around post st on previous row.

Back   Front

← Post of Stitch

Front loop—front lp Back loop—back lp

Front Loop   Back Loop

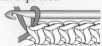

Half double crochet—hdc: Yo, insert hook in st, yo, pull through st, yo, pull through all 3 lps on hook.

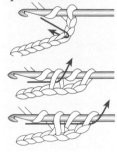

Double crochet—dc: Yo, insert hook in st, yo, pull through st, [yo, pull through 2 lps] twice.

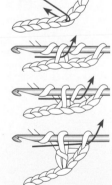

Change colors: Drop first color; with 2nd color, pull through last 2 lps of st.

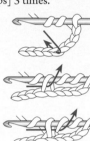

Treble crochet—tr: Yo twice, insert hook in st, yo, pull through st, [yo, pull through 2 lps] 3 times.

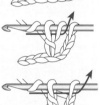

Double treble crochet—dtr: Yo 3 times, insert hook in st, yo, pull through st, [yo, pull through 2 lps] 4 times.

Single crochet decrease (sc dec): (Insert hook, yo, draw lp through) in each of the sts indicated, yo, draw through all lps on hook.

Example of 2-sc dec

Half double crochet decrease (hdc dec): (Yo, insert hook, yo, draw lp through) in each of the sts indicated, yo, draw through all lps on hook.

Example of 2-hdc dec

Double crochet decrease (dc dec): (Yo, insert hook, yo, draw loop through, draw through 2 lps on hook) in each of the sts indicated, yo, draw through all lps on hook.

Example of 2-dc dec

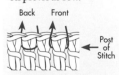

Example of 2-tr dec

Treble crochet decrease (tr dec): Holding back last lp of each st, tr in each of the sts indicated, yo, pull through all lps on hook.

US		UK
sl st (slip stitch)	=	sc (single crochet)
sc (single crochet)	=	dc (double crochet)
hdc (half double crochet)	=	htr (half treble crochet)
dc (double crochet)	=	tr (treble crochet)
tr (treble crochet)	=	dtr (double treble crochet)
dtr (double treble crochet)	=	ttr (triple treble crochet)
skip	=	miss